THE PRACTICE OF PERSONAL TRANSFORMATION

A Jungian Approach

by

Strephon Kaplan Williams

Other Journey Press books by Strephon Kaplan Williams

In general distribution in book stores and by mail order from Journey Press

The Jungian-Senoi Dreamwork Manual.
320 pages, illustrations, over 35 major dreamwork methods. The standard work in the field used in many colleges and growth centers throughout the world. $15.95 plus $2.00 postage and handling.

Sources - Synchronicity Readings for Dealing with Life's Issues.
96 pages. A pocket size book of 64 source readings which are chosen synchronistically to give new awareness about personal choices and issues. $3.95 plus $1.00 postage and handling.

Seedbursts - Spiritual Aphorisms for Life Change.
128 pages, beautifully printed with principles on such areas as relationship, love, choice, consciousness, healing and comic relief. $6.95 plus $2.00 postage and handling.

Private limited editions through Journey Press only.

Transforming Childhood.
over 60 lessons on processing various aspects of childhood such as the wounded child, the wondrous child, birth and rebirth, and graduating from childhood. Used in the Jungian-Senoi Institute's Transforming Childhood series of workshops. $14.95 plus $2.00 postage and handling.

The Healing Archetypes.
Strephon Kaplan Williams' Unified Field Theory of the Archetypes with extensive illustrations and text on how archetypes work in life and in the personality. $14.95 plus $2.00 postage and handling.

Journeys - A Newsletter for Spiritual and Psychological Growth.
12 issues a year. Various topics and exercises from Institute workshop teaching. $36, includes postage and handling.

To order from Journey Press, send a check made out to Journey Press for the price of the book and postage and handling. California residents please add 6 % sales tax. Your orders will be processed within a week. Prices subject to change without notice. Thank you.

Send to:
Journey Press-2
P.O. Box 9036
Berkeley, CA 94709

THE PRACTICE OF PERSONAL TRANSFORMATION

A Jungian Approach

The Book About Transformational Psychology That Wrote Itself

by

Strephon Kaplan Williams

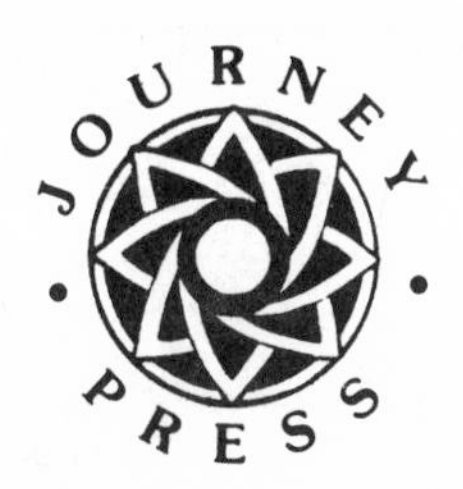

JOURNEY PRESS
Berkeley, California

Acknowledgement

First, to the Life Source itself as it has inspired me and many others I have shared with over the years.

Second, to my own specific teachers from the past, my mother, Gene Derwood, my first analyst, Rebekah Earle, and Elizabeth Boyden Howes and Sheila Moon, analysts and teachers, and to Dorothea Romankiw, another teacher and friend for me.

Third, to the significant male and female companions of my life who have shared a deep sense of spiritual journey with me. I include especially my friends Joyce Perry and Terran Daily.

Fourth, to Terran Harcourt Daily, my psychology editor and advisor, and to Luz Mena, Institute and Journey Press coordinator extraordinaire. To Judy Bess, my fine text editor, and to Sebastian Orfali, founder-editor of And/Or Press, without whom I would not be in the publishing business. Also to Scott, word processor, and finally to John of Berkeley Computer who has kept my Kaypro 10 going all these years with fine service and warmth.

Edition: 9 8 7 6 5 4 3 2 1

Library of Congress card catalog number: 85-80472
ISBN 0-918572-29-0

You may order single copies prepaid direct from the publisher for $9.95 plus $1.00 postage and handling. California residents add $0.60 sales tax. Bay area residents add $0.05 more to the above. Your order will usually be processed in one day.

JOURNEY PRESS

P.O.BOX 9036
BERKELEY, CA 94709

FOR LIMITED EDITION ONLY:
First hundred copies signed and numbered by the author

AUTHOR'S SIGNATURE: NUMBER:

Judy Bess text editor
Sebastian Orfali publishing consultant
Jani Beckwith graphic design
Strephon Williams illustrations
distribution by Bookpeople, Publisher's Group West and other distributors.
typesetting by BerkeleyType

Training and workshops available in dreamwork and Jungian psychology. Please write for further details.

Dedicated to Joyce Perry,
whose personal journey is
a living example of this process.
Her work has helped enrich these pages,
even though her story is not given here specifically.

A Personal Note

This is the book that wrote itself. As author I was tricked by my own unconscious. For originally I thought I was writing the introduction for another book, **The Healing Archetypes,** but what transpired was a complete outpouring in itself. My material just took off. I seemed to be writing day and night, feeling an onrush of principles, thoughts, feelings and examples as I let my pen do the work. This book is a being that wanted to exist, an unexpected pregnancy that slipped into my writing schedule, which I have otherwise planned for years ahead.

I welcome what has come through me, a transmission about what it is to live life. I do and I do not take personal responsibility for what is written here. The material goes beyond what I am able to live yet, and so I myself become its reader like anyone else. After the heat of the writing I am glad to join you as reader and I myself work on the practice of personal transformation.

I do not apologize for using the words "transformation" and "transformational." Some "New Age" commentators come down on words which have achieved a place in the language of growing people, as if a word can ever be used too much. When said and meant from the heart, no word ever becomes out of date. And in a like vein, you can say a word and that will not be enough to affect you. We practice what we say and we say what we practice. Mind and idea need not be separate from body and soul. In terms of wholeness the word and the action are one.

Shalom,

Strephon Kaplan Williams
June 3, 1985

A Note On the Writing Style

A simplified style is expressed here. Only commas, periods, question marks and exclamation points are used in the text to clarify meanings and indicate pauses. "They" and "their" may be utilized as non-sexist singular pronouns. Bold face is frequently resorted to for heightening content.

Preface by Judy Bess

When I was invited to work on this book I had never heard of Strephon Williams, the Jungian psychologist. I envisioned an emaciated intellectual writing convoluted prose in a cavernous room.

Instead I found an overgrown garden cottage, a toy monkey climbing over the back fence, a man with a strong and subtle presence, and a manuscript that drew me in from the first word.

It turned out to be one of those books that speaks precisely to what is most alive and conscious in me.

The writing is alive. The ideas are alive. Old familiar concepts and techniques are turned inside out and illuminated. Notice, for example, how the concept of ego becomes an immediate experience.

And the use of affirmations. Perhaps you, like me, have had negative results with statements such as "Money flows into my life abundantly," which, lacking a basis in reality, merely reinforce one's skepticism. Strephon's affirmations are different. They are carefully written to express truths, real potentials that already exist. They don't tell us to make something true by believing it (which I suspect does work for some people). Instead each one formulates some actual truth that you are choosing to align with in spite of your inner skeptic. So what makes them work is choice, not belief. And I personally can use them to change my inner, and thence my outer, reality.

As editor, I corrected and improved Strephon's prose. Usually he was flexible, even appreciative. But sometimes he just wouldn't change those strangely worded sentences that jar the expectations, or the sudden questions that seem tangential to what's being discussed. After a while I caught on. It's not supposed to be smooth reading. It's designed to get you to stop, attend, ask yourself questions, write in the margin. This is a book to read with your yellow marker ready and your journal at hand.

There have been synchronicity and serendipity throughout this effort, but the most striking incident occurred last night. I had previously written a preface to this book that seemed good enough at first, but on second reading stank. So I was assigned to rewrite it. I worked on it for days, writing page after page, rejecting most, distilling some. Now it was midnight, and the deadline was 9:30 am. I had only three acceptable sentences, and my mind was blank. Empty. I just could not come up with any more. I was exhausted. What could I contribute anyway? I was falling asleep. Was it time to throw in the sponge and admit failure? I was ready. But was this the regressive pull? I would at least consult Strephon's Synchronicity Readings before giving up. I tossed the coins and the number I got was 46:

What is needed is commitment and courage
The situation will not be overcome unless you risk everything in the struggle.
If you are unwilling to push through you will suffer a loss anyway.
Maximum effort and devotion may well tip the scales in a favorable direction.

I woke up. "O.K.," I wrote in my journal. "Up all night if that's what it takes." I made some tea, put on some music, and got to work. So here I am, the sky getting lighter, the birds starting to sing, my battle waged, this preface done.

Judy Bess, text editor
5 am, May 29, 1985

TABLE OF CONTENTS

The Practices 73

PART VI—SOURCES—SYNCHRONICITY READINGS FOR LIFE CHANGE 217
Sixty-four psychic readings on key life issues and dynamics, which came to the author in a dream vision. Readers formulate questions and choose a number synchronistically to obtain the number of the reading to be applied to the issue. A Source tool in action.

PART I

THE WAY OF TRANSFORMATION

THE WAY OF TRANSFORMATION

How we live our lives is up to ourselves alone, but what comes our way in life indicates another and wiser force at work in our own journeys and in the world.

I believe in a bright future, both for myself and for others, but this future cannot occur unless we choose it to occur, unless we choose the Way of Healing, which I also call the Way of Transformation.

What is the Way of Transformation? We can look around in the world and, if we dare, in our own lives, and see that there are many things not right from our own points of view. We could even see this life as primarily a place of illness against which we must continually fight. Many of us, myself included, have felt the need to rid ourselves of conflict, frustration, pain and illness, while still not changing ourselves enough. We are trying to change the world and those around us without changing ourselves.

This gets us down to basic principles. Throughout this book you will be presented with principles for how to better live life. The first one is, **To change the world or those around you, change yourself first.** What does this mean? It says to me that first I can change myself, that I am rich in inner resources if I will only focus sufficiently on who I am and what I can accomplish in life.

This book is about fulfillment, if nothing else. It is about effectiveness in life, but probably not from a traditional point of view, or from the picture you now have of life.

Today many of us are searching for a new and better way of going through life. We are experiencing a change of consciousness and experiencing what it means to be effective in the world. **To be effective we must know reality.** This is one of our major tasks. How we see others and ourselves, how we perceive life energy determines our choices and our goals in life. If you want to deal with your problems you have to face reality, all of it, leaving nothing out.

We look inward to look outward. This is the new revolution for consciousness. Everywhere on this planet people are talking, on long walks, in public forums, in books and periodicals, and especially in close, personal situations among friends and workmates. People are talking and eighty percent of what they are saying is a constant reflecting upon themselves and their lives.

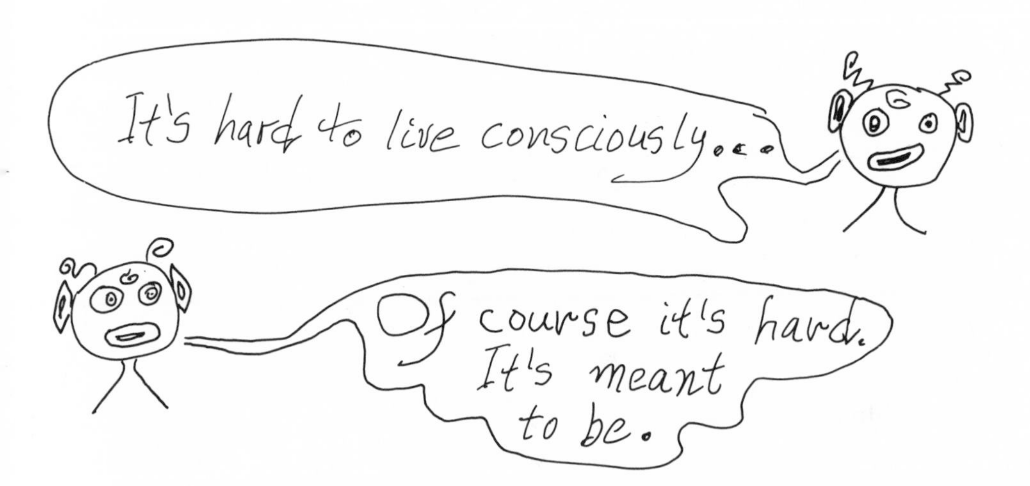

The Inward Revolution

This is the Inward Revolution. This is the new focus in life. This is the new frontier.

We turn inward to turn outward. It is from within that the new potential, the new perception, the new possibility for healing comes. As we look inward we become aware of an intuitive voice which provides a reliable source of direction for our lives. This is the voice of the Self, the Central Archetype, that which integrates and transforms our lives if we will only listen and interact with it. Within each of us is a tremendous resource for meaning and healing which has always been there and which has been, whether we know it or not, responsible for how far we have gotten in our lives.

But we have resisted this Source Energy, become confused by it and afraid to allow it its direction in our choices and our being in the world. Now we can change all that. Now we can get our principles straight. Now we can develop that which makes us truly alive.

Although we want to experience life, vitality and love for ourselves, each other, and the world, most of us are still seeking something else which we never find. We are still trying to control and make things happen which are strictly to our own benefit. We are still trying to stave off fear, fear that things will not go right, fear that things will not go our way. We are still trying to make ourselves happy, not realizing that happiness and joy are outcomes of the Way instead of goals in life.

And things will never go the way we want them to unless we both change what we want and want what comes our way. The problem is to know what life wants of you as well as to know how to be effective in life.

Within ourselves is a Center, a tremendous resource for dealing with the world if we can only understand and actively relate to this resource.

Thus, **the greatest treasure on earth becomes yourself.**

We shall not get caught in spiritual emptiness or fixation on all the known goals in the world which everybody wants.You would like a good and fulfilling job, a warm and intimate relationship, children who don't make serious mistakes in life, financial stability, a nice house on a piece of property you can call your own, to know what the future is going to be like? These things are definitely possible, but only to a certain extent. **To the degree that we try to control the outcome in life, to that same degree will we lack fullness.**

Fullness in life comes through letting go to life, not controlling it, and this is one great metaphysical secret we shall be dealing with here. It is never the specifics we want, the concrete goals. **Always want the process and let the goals take care of themselves.** We do not commit ourselves to goals but to a process which may bring us toward our goals. Many of us are strong in goals and weak in process. We would like all sorts of things out of life but resist realizing that what we get out of life is what happens now, not later. If you would build for security later, you must become secure now. You do not wait for The One to love. You love the one you relate to now. You build the future by full immersion in the present. You make your choices in the Now, in present reality.

We need a change in attitude, we need many changes in attitude. It is not enough to change your wardrobe, your job, your place of residence, your lifestyle, your friends, to have a change of heart toward life.

The Choice—a Change of Heart

This change of heart is what we are after. All sorts of attitudes, of ways we see life, will go in the fires of our own transformation. It is as if we have now been invited to a great feast but are we ready? Will we indeed let ourselves enter the room and partake? Will we know what we are doing? Will we sit in the smallest place, or a place closer to center?

This book can help show the way to that feast. We need be stuck no longer in inner poverty and immersed in compulsions and cries for help. We can enter the room.

This book is written as a handbook for personal transformation toward a life of fullness and dynamic vitality. In brief, this book is about self-fulfillment through relationship to the real sources of life. The words and drawings present principles and their application to every-day living as well as to our more ultimate spiritual quest. They come out of my own experience of working with myself and others in practicing what has been meaningful in our lives. We work with the personal inspiration of our dreams, with source energies directly experienced in our lives, with life-principles embedded in many spiritual traditions, with central experiences that reveal when our actions have been in tune with the way life is.

We describe a new image of a person who really is alive to him or herself and others, of a person who has all the fears, enthusiasms and feelings which most of us have, yet who deals more and more effectively with life as it really is. And we see in you, as well as in ourselves, an inner radiance, at once individual and universal in its application to life.

This is the Source, the Self, as the great Swiss psychologist, C.G. Jung, described it. We have elaborated on his psychology, refined and added to his perspective here and there. We have included formulations in principles and exercises to make the material usable to all.

We are the people already living many aspects of this journey, as well as myself the author who formulated this material. You can see us as an ever widening circle of hands with a common center and purpose for living life on this earth. Can you also begin to visualize yourself included within the circle?

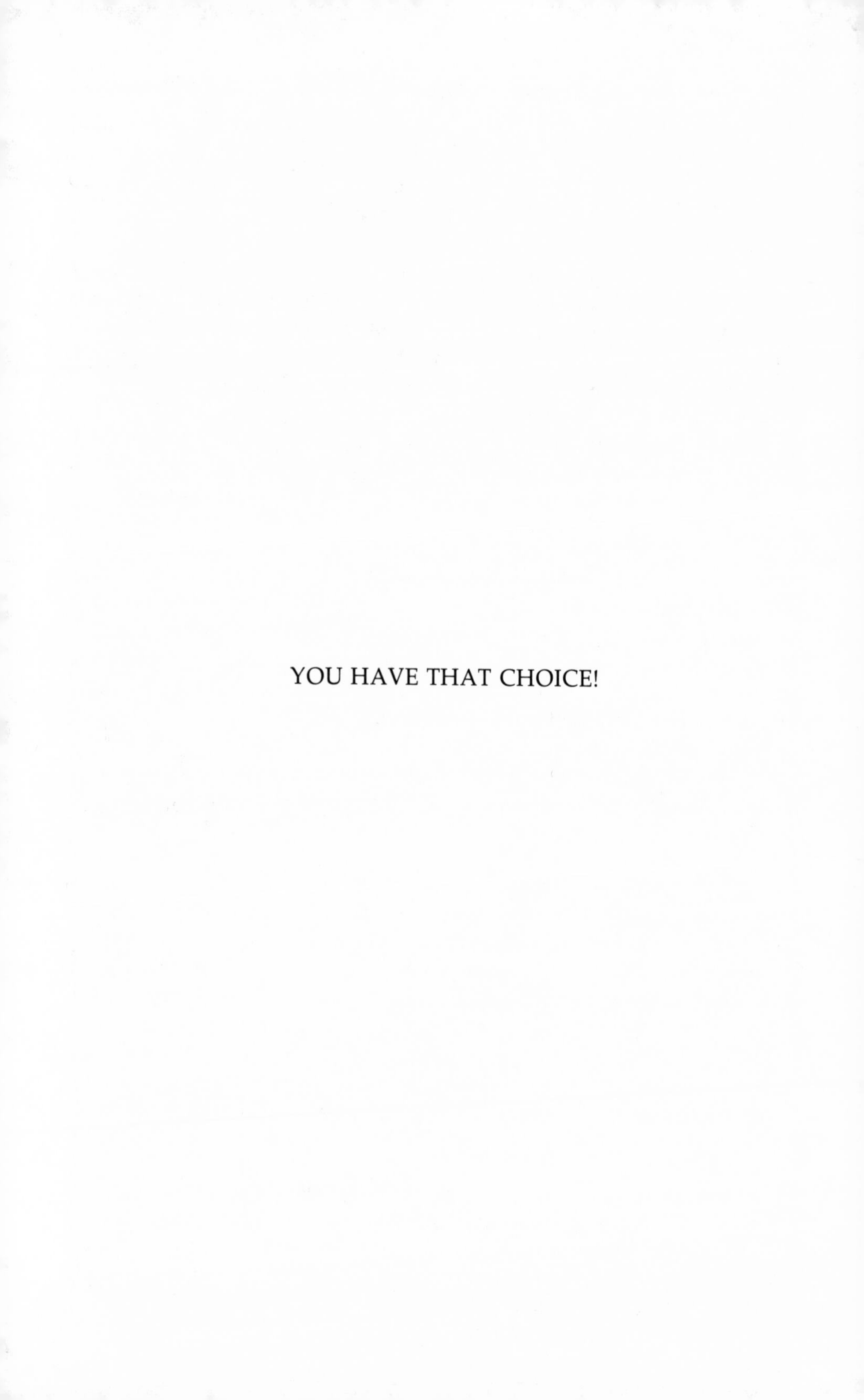

YOU HAVE THAT CHOICE!

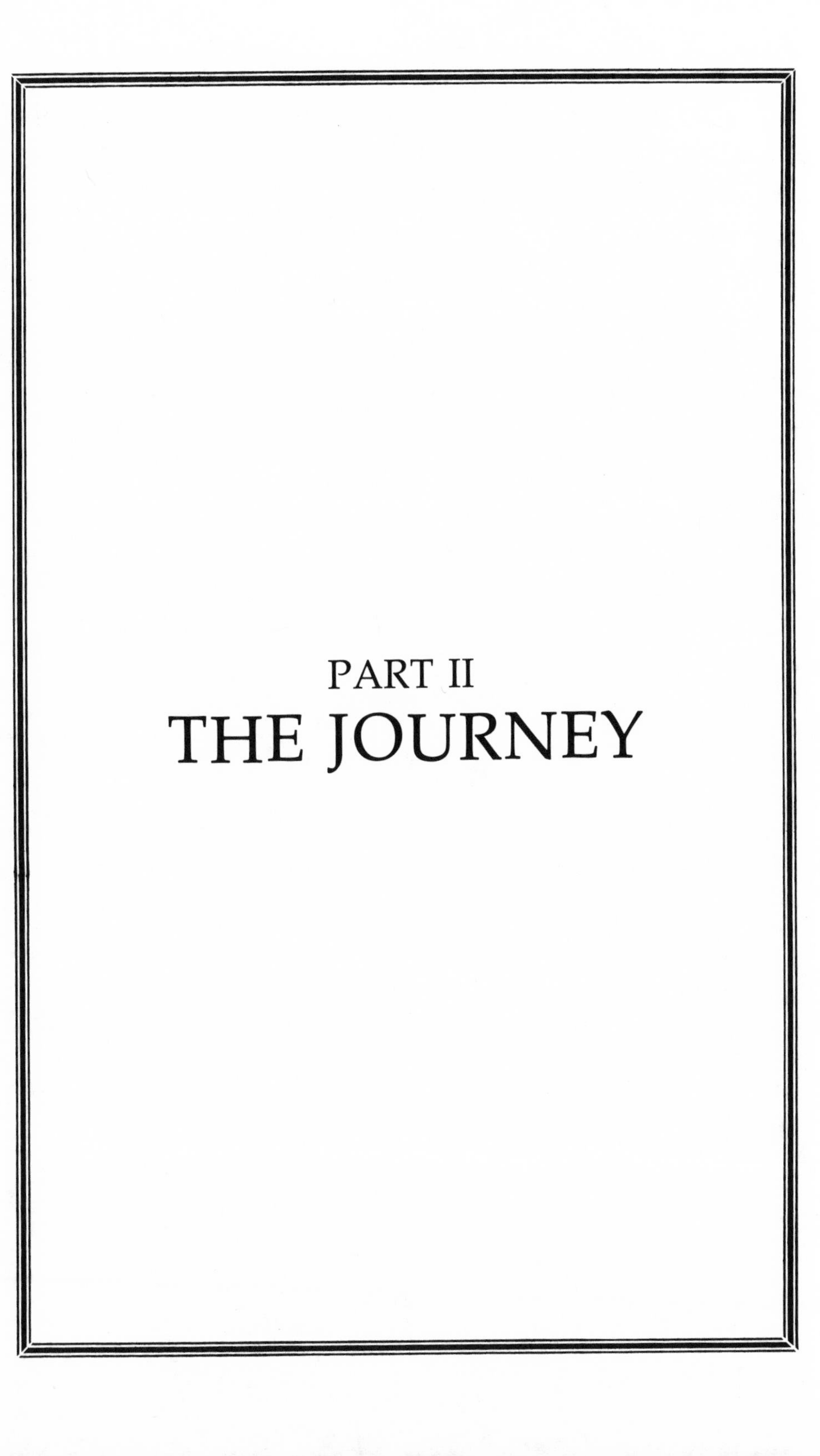

PART II
THE JOURNEY

We Are Not What We Seem

Did you ever wake up to a new day and for an instant not know where you were or who you are?

All of us have had this experience but usually we switch in to some known images and values of who we are.

I am a man, age twenty-three. I am a woman, age thirty-five. I have a name, Jamie Loren. I am a Democrat. I am a Republican. I am a mother. I have three thousand dollars in the bank.

Or, I am a nobody, just a guy or gal trying to get along in the world, have a few beers, read popular novels, go to the movies, cash my paycheck every week and float. None of this growth stuff for me. I'm not upwardly mobile. I don't even know what it means.

Why not for a moment quickly define yourself and see what you come up with? List about seven "I am..." sentences, if you can. Choose to do this now.

1.

2.

3.

4.

5.

6.

7.

What does this exercise point out to you? For one thing, the futility of defining oneself, as we all know from social occasions where someone we have never met starts asking us questions about who we are and what we do.

Who I am determines how I live life.

So it is healthy to always take another look at oneself to see where one is going in life. The plain fact is that we tend to define ourselves by identifying with images we have of ourselves or others have of us. And behind these identity images and roles are **archetypes**.

Archetypes Are the Innate Energies of the Universe

Archetype (pronounced ark-a-type) is an ancient Greek word meaning original imprinter. Just as there is an original typeface for making and remaking each letter of these words, there is also an original mold, or pre-form, which determines how we and life operate.

If I wake up in the morning and immediately think of what I am going to make for my children's breakfast I am identifying myself as a mother, I am identifying myself with the mother archetype, an aspect of the universal archetype of the Feminine, of which the mother role and image is one of the forms.

And in the same way a man with a child will identify with a form of the Masculine archetype when he calls himself a father and demands that a child finish his or her chores.

Of course there are many forms and roles which express the archetype of the Masculine, roles such as lover, warrior, or businessman.

And for a female human being, some common roles are the attractive woman, the lover, the supporter, the good friend to others, the businesswoman.

We are our roles and yet we are not our roles.

This book is about archetypes and transformation because we believe that people like ourselves become all mixed up in their roles and images of themselves and so tend to lose much which is life.

A classic example is identification with parental roles. Many men and women see themselves primarily as parents.

Then when their children grow up and go out into the world, they are left with little which is fulfilling to do. We all know how certain parents, still identified with being fathers or mothers, and still seeing their grown-up family members as children, spend their lives in such activities as calling up their younger family members and trying to give them advice on how to live life.

Always get your own rooms in order first. You never know when you will be called upon to become a guest in your own house.

What does this mean to you?

We all have a great tendency toward trying to evaluate and fix up other people's lives to the neglect of our own.

We project what has not yet been made conscious.

We so easily get sucked into other people's lives and events because of projection. **Projection is putting out there what is really inside ourselves.** Projection is one of the greatest evidences that the archetypes really exist.

If we look again at the mother archetype we will probably have noticed that at various times in our lives we have seen someone else besides our biological mother as a mother for us.

Certain positive attributes of the mother role and archetype include nurturing, opening, giving, and understanding. But there are also negative attributes of the mother archetype, such as being devouring, irrational, instinctually messy, to list a few.These latter are often well described in fairy tales and usually less talked about in families than the positive traits. Cinderella was always cleaning up after her messy sisters. The witch wants to put Hansel and Gretel into her oven. Mothers and other men and women who let go of their bodies and become overweight are in the grip of the Great Mother, the devouring maw which cannot stop compulsively eating. Unconscious identification with the mother archetype is not a good thing.

We may project either positive or negative mother traits which are really inside ourselves. We may actually project onto those who also have these traits which are inside ourselves. An overweight person is overweight and is also a good person to project positive or negative mother onto.

Projecting the Unconscious

We project what has not yet been made conscious.

What does this mean?

Essentially, if I have left home feeling only partly fulfilled by my actual mother, I will seek people as lovers, teachers and friends who actively express mothering qualities I did not get in childhood. I project onto them from my own need for a mother and they in turn act out the mother role for me until both or either of us cannot stand it anymore.

Projection is necessary but eventually harmful because we are "giving away" a part of ourselves which we need for our own integration and wholeness.

This may sound wildly impossible, but each of us, whether male or female, has both feminine and masculine attributes within. In growing up, males tend to identify with masculine traits and pursuits and females with feminine traits and pursuits. But this is not wholeness, one of the great goals in life.

It is true that culture helps determine the roles we play out, but these same roles also have an archetypal base. We need roles to express archetypal energies. Some jobs and roles, for example, are more nurturing, while others are more decisive. We need to be creative with the roles, neither rejecting them nor identifying with them. Either sex can wear an earring in the ear or not wear earrings at all. The earring stands for an adornment of beauty from the feminine archetype. Men wearing an ear ring could be stating that they as well as the female have a love of beauty and adornment.

Likewise, dresses are more flowing and free than most pants, and therefore give more a feeling of the feminine. Women today can wear either pants or skirts and feel different according to what they are wearing. Men have not yet gotten into wearing skirts, except in a few cultures, although many of the ancient men wore them all the time.

Most people want to fit into their culture, so they dress appropriately to the culture. If they dress too unusually, people will see them as different from themselves, and project dark energy, the shadow, onto them, sometimes with severe consequences.

We Are Not Males And Females—We Are Persons

Think about it for a moment. In your own childhood family you may have experienced your father as more nurturing in some ways than your mother. And your mother may have been more decisive, and of the masculine quality, than your father.

It is well and good to develop all archetypes within myself.

I am and can become a person in this life. A person is not identified with one sex only but seeks to develop all sides of him- or herself.

There are three sexes. Two are males and females who unconsciously live their biological roles mostly identified with them and with the archetypes of masculine and feminine behind the roles. The third sex are those persons, whether biologically male or female, who consciously develop and integrate both masculine and feminine within themselves. This third type I call persons.

Sex does not determine personhood, it only influences it.

The Love Projection

Most of us have fallen in love at least once in our lives, and for many it was a great experience—wonderful in its ecstasy and terrible in its suffering if there was also a fall.

Again, in the love projection we put out there onto the other person what is really inside ourselves. And we must project first before we can integrate. Don't be too embarrassed by having fallen in love.

The psychological dynamic of projection is,

We identify with one archetype and project its opposite.

As a young man I may naturally identify with being a male, one who is biologically and socially aggressive, definite and goal-oriented. But because I am identified with these dynamics I will project out onto a woman my feminine dynamics of softness, flow, beauty and openness. The woman in turn who is attracted to me will be identified with certain feminine characteristics and project onto her man the inner masculine.

If the relationship develops and they find themselves in bed together making love, how can they resist it? Then each of them through the sexual expression will experience their own opposite in the other.

The woman will experience herself as receiving dynamic and decisive energy, among other things. And the man will experience himself receiving warmth, flow and beauty, things he may not obtain that much, for instance, in his work situation.

Have you ever thought of why sex is so powerful for most people including yourself?

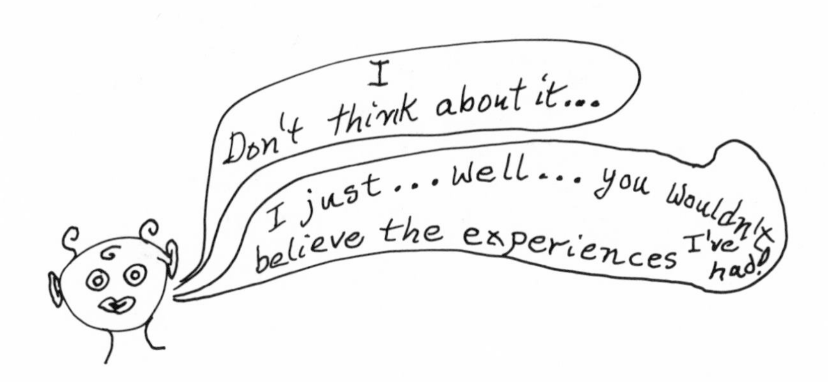

The Central Archetype of the Self

Sex certainly has its physical components, the heightened awareness and energy flow, the tension building and releasing which helps create and warm up a relationship and sometimes leads to making babies.

But seen archetypally sex is the experience of the uniting of opposites, expressing the most central archetype in the whole of existence.

This is the **Central Archetype of the Self,** the archetype of unity and harmony in the universe. Is there any wonder that it is this expression which leads to conceiving babies and creating the next generation?

Experiences of unity are celebrated not only sexually of course. There are family and class reunions, hugs between friends, marriage ceremonies, peace-making treaties and new contracts between labor and management. All these and many other life expressions have in common new unity through resolving conflicts between parties involved.

THE GOAL OF LIFE IS WHOLENESS AND THE WAY TO THE GOAL IS THE PRACTICE OF BRINGING RESOLUTION TO ALL CONFLICTS. THIS IS THE PRACTICE OF PERSONAL TRANSFORMATION.

The Nature of Healing

What is healing and why do we all need it?

True, I may not at the moment be suffering from cancer or any other dread disease. But the severe forms of illness, whether physical or mental, serve to illustrate the universal fact of sickness and its healing.

Sickness is a part of us at odds with itself and in need of change and resolution. Sickness in life means conflict, means a clash of opposing views and values, of opposing tendencies and conflicting energies.

We are all in need of healing each day because each day we have become one-sided and in opposition to some part of ourselves or others.

And because we need healing each day of our lives we need, all of us, to develop the skills for healing which include **sacrifice** and **bringing resolution**. And out of this process then, a new transformation occurs, a change of personality and being.

Sacrifice is our voluntarily choosing to let go of what we are holding on to. What we do not voluntarily sacrifice will be taken from us anyway.

I choose in every moment to let go of that which would prevent living the greatest value in that moment.

We so often do not like to sacrifice, to let go and change, because we have strong attitudes which constantly say,

* "What is mine belongs to me forever," or
* "What I have now is better than what I can get in the future."

Not so! These attitudes are ultimately life defeating since they make us hold onto the present and try to control the future without giving up the past.

The way to life is to let go of the past, to be fully present in the present so that the future may be born.

If you don't want to practice sacrifice in your life, why don't you try the opposite technique? Try hard to hold onto everything you hold dear. Never give up anything unless it is absolutely ripped out of your hands. And then add to your possessions new objects of desire whenever you can so that your life can always be full up to the brim and overflowing.

And what is our daily task so that we may have new life? Each one says it in his or her own words as intentions, as commitments to actions.

"I will let go of anything I cling to so that I and others may have new life."

"For the coming month I will give up holding on to my anger without resolving it."

"I will acknowledge my successes but not dwell on them this coming week."

Not to continually let go of both the positive and the negative as they arrive in life, no strangers to our door, is to create cisterns of unresolved energy which will explode out on us at the oddest and most inappropriate moments.

Sacrifice prepares us for healing, and bringing or allowing resolution creates the healing.

As in physical healing the surgeon cuts away the torn and sick flesh so that the body can create new tissue which closes the wound and makes the person whole again.

Healing is sacrifice and bringing resolution, out of which the new can be born. All nature, including ourselves, exists in conflict which leads to change. A good part of each day is spent by each of us as individuals, groups, and even countries, in trying to creatively resolve issues and conflicts.

Conflicts are natural to existence. There is always a hero and an adversary in every situation. Sometimes we are the good guys and sometimes we are the bad guys, depending on who is doing the evaluating.

This is what we mean when we say that all conflicts are made up of opposites and are therefore archetypal (pronounced ark-ka-type-al). One side feels one way and the other side feels the opposite way.

Conflicts in human affairs are the equivalent of sickness in bodily situations. When we are physically sick we assume we must get well, so we go to the doctor. When nation states are in conflict they do not assume they are sick and need healing. The United Nations could be the physician to the world but the arrogant and powerful among nations will not put their wounds at a healer's feet. It all amounts to each side seeing themselves as right and the other side as wrong.

The Enemy Is Within

What can this statement mean to you? For most of us it says that we each experience internal splits within ourselves. Remember when we described how we all tend to identify with one archetypal opposite in life and project the other? Well, if I identify with only one side of myself, say, the nurturing and flowing qualities of the feminine, then when I get into a situation where I need to be decisive and aggressive, qualities of the masculine, I may not be able to express these well, if at all, and therefore I am in conflict.

The Need For Resolution

Conflicts are the battlegrounds of the opposites. All conflicts need resolution eventually.

The term **resolution** is a wonderful word for healing because it describes a process of ending conflicts by creating new unities out of the opposites involved in the struggle.

Resolution means bringing opposites together to form a new unity.

All well and good, you say, but how is this done? I look around me and I see everyone, including nations, in conflict, and with little getting resolved.

As a realist I would say you are probably right. **Most people live and die in more conflicts than they ever resolve.**

MOST PEOPLE DO NOT CONSCIOUSLY RESOLVE CONFLICTS. THEY REPRESS THEM.

Sad but true. **Repression is the act of hiding from ourselves one or more opposites in a conflict.** Most people repress sides of themselves by rejecting one opposite and identifying with the other.

This revelation still amazes me! If I have an attitude that anger is bad I will repress my anger by identifying with the calm, kind side of myself. I see myself as only kind and gentle in any situation and suppress all tendencies to attack or defend myself against others. I will not be able to meet certain of my needs.

One-sided repression of an important life energy will not work in the long run. Extremely independent or autonomous people may tend to get cancer, creating a situation in which everyone has to take care of and worry over them. They repress their own vulnerability, thus eventually creating it in the extreme. Anger-repressed people make others angry with them because of their one-sidedness. People who make a virtue out of wearing a perpetual smile do subtle things which make others angry. They may say they will do something for you and then not come through. Since they are repressing anger they have a hard time being direct and saying No.They are unconsciously angry at themselves for being unable to refuse things not in their own interest. So they make you angry at them instead.

Repression does not ultimately resolve conflicts. It only makes them more extreme when they finally burst out.

In order for healing to occur we must continually sacrifice our one-sidedness and choose to become whole in the situation. We must express both opposites and experience the conflict fully for healing to manifest.

I am more and more able to experience the natural conflicts in my life and to bring them to resolution.

How many of us can choose to live this basic principle in our lives starting today?

The other major way people and nations tend to deal with conflicts is to balance power with power until the situation at last explodes and they both try to defeat and utterly annihilate each other.

Many couples and families are ripe arenas for seeing how conflicts are dealt with from a power basis. The father may try to dominate one way, and the mother in other usually more indirect ways. The children grow up feeling the effects of this power struggle because most parents try to win all the power fights with their children. One time when my eldest daughter was four she insisted on climbing some stairs I was building and fell down and hurt herself. In my repressed fear and overt anger I slapped her on the top of her head. She told me, "Daddies shouldn't hit their children." Well, I was mad enough to. I wanted her to obey. She wanted to test her own power, which she has been doing ever since. I learned that when my children said No, they did not want to eat a certain food, they did not have to eat that food. I was brought up to eat what was before me. I was defeated in my own choices at every turn. It all starts in childhood. The patterns played out there in millions of lives infect or heal the nation.

Trying to overcome power with power is no way to resolve conflicts. It only exacerbates or makes them worse.

And what about nation states? History too often shows us that nations tend to hate rival nations and to war and compete against them. Seeing the rival nation as bad and the enemy while seeing oneself as good and a friend to all is an example again of trying to resolve conflicts by identifying with one opposite and repressing, and therefore denying, the other.

Nations as well as individuals repress the "bad" and identify with the "good." And what is the good? What each person or nation identifies with and calls the good. One segment of the population sees abortion as criminal because it kills a potential human life. Another segment sees forcing a woman to bring an unwanted child into the world as a crime against both her and the child. Both factions feel right through identification with their own positions, and identification with one opposite make the other opposite wrong in most people's minds. Yet within the pro-abortionist is the agonized mother who has lost her child, and within the "right-to-life" person may be the secret life-taker who supports increasing armaments and moving to the edge of mass destruction.

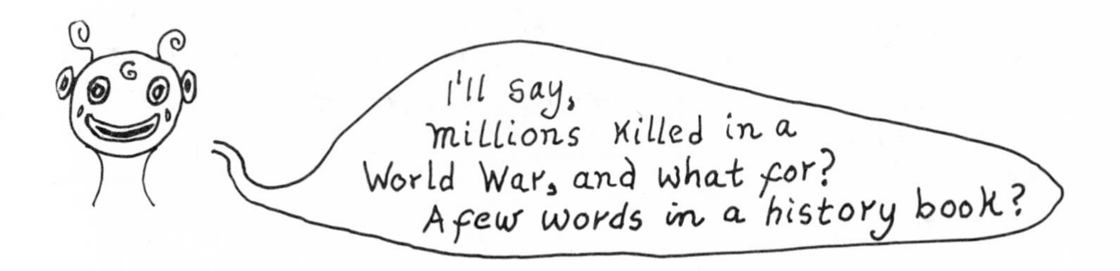

Repression as well as identification causes projection.

When we repress a side of ourselves we project it out onto something or someone else. This is called a **shadow** projection, in which we project the enemy onto someone else. It has been the source of tremendous and unnecessary destructiveness in families, relationships, organizations and nations.

We are now at a period in our own lives and in the life of the world in which we can deal with and make conscious this dangerous game of projecting the opposite.

I am the opposite I project. I am not just what I identify with and see as myself.

To say it still once more so that we may all begin to get it and live its message, **We identify with one opposite and project the other.** We can either project an opposite quality, such as the masculine if I am identified with the feminine, or we can project a negative quality such as the shadow if I am identified with a good quality, my persona.

Healing means bringing resolution. What if all nations and peoples took as their primary guiding context by which they lived, the principle of bringing creative resolution to all conflicts both big and small? What a transformation would occur in the world then!

A creative resolution is a unifying of opposites out of which new life is born.

A false or non-creative resolution would be one in which one opposite seemingly annihilates the other thereby ending, at least for the moment, the conflict.

Annihilating your opponent only gives you a temporary reprieve from your conflict. You may breathe again but the conditions which created the conflict in the first place have not been adequately dealt with and you will inevitably create a new conflict for yourself.

When couples develop natural conflicts, annihilating one's partner by leaving the relationship may not solve much in a final sense. **What you leave behind will appear in front of you at the next gate.** What you have not resolved in one relationship you will create for yourself in the next. Besides, **if you can say No in a relationship you do not have to say No to the relationship.**

I seek to resolve all issues and conflicts in my life as they come up.

We are hopeful. This book is about archetypes, about the natural opposites in ourselves and in existence. This book is also about healing, about the possibility of bringing resolution to conflicts as they come up in life. And ultimately this book is about personal transformation, that meaningful change of life and personality which inevitably occurs when we practice the art of creative resolution in our lives.

Focusing

To help in retraining your consciousness, remember to ask yourself these questions in all aspects of your daily life.

1. Do I choose to deal with conflict or to avoid it with easy solutions and unrealistic beliefs?

2. Do I choose to accept all of reality as it is or do I choose to repress things I am uncomfortable with?

3. Do I choose to see as within myself all projections as they become known to me or do I choose to continue seeing as outside myself dynamics which are really within?

4. Do I choose to disidentify from any opposites or dynamics once they are known to me?

5. Do I choose to integrate the opposites in my life on a daily basis? Or do I choose to stay one-sided, identifying with the right and rejecting the wrong?

6. Do I choose personal transformation in my life as a daily practice?

I must continually ask myself questions to become real. I must doubt who I am to know that I exist. If I want conscious integration I must choose for it continuously. Our suggestion is that you write out these questions and say them to yourself at least once a week.

The Practice of Personal Transformation

Transformation is total revolution in the psyche, is total change in one's life, yet if this scares you, consider first the reality of existence.

Heraclitus, the ancient Greek philosopher, said it centuries ago, **All is change.**

To resist change is to create change in the extreme. To go with change and use the energy is to practice the principle of acceptance. To choose change also is to practice the principle of sacrificing the old to create new life.

Yet change for change's sake is not the goal. Yes, all is change, but this kind of cosmic process reflects how the opposites, the archetypes, work their ever-moving bouncing back and forth of dualities, the cosmic interchange and constant re-balancing of contraries, sometimes leading to new unities and sometimes not. What consciousness brings to this process is getting ourselves unstuck from one opposite so that we can relate to both, and helping evoke new unities which otherwise might not occur.

In comes the principle and law of transformation, of breeding out of old oppositions new unities which create total revolution in the whole.

To change the part, change the whole.

Let us face ourselves squarely in the human condition. I work with so many people who come in wanting just to change one thing, but experience fear and the desire to withdraw when they find out from their own processes that total change is more what is needed.

A Conversation

"Yes, I want to resolve this conflict in myself but I also want to stay the way I am."

"You do?"

"Yes. Dear God, fix me up but let me keep what I already have."

"You want to stay the way you are, yet want to change?"

"Well, I want to keep the good stuff, of course. I would be more willing to give up the bad stuff, the old hang-ups, the old problems."

'You want to change yet you don't want to change the good things?"

"Do I have to change everything? You are asking too great a price."

"You said it. You alone know what you have to do."

"But what if I don't make it? What if my whole world falls apart?"

"Where did you get that attitude?"

"Well, won't it fall apart?"

"You can try and see. Ask yourself what have you got to lose? Do you like yourself and your life the way you are?"

"Well, no. That's why I came to see you."

"I can't make you change. No one can get you to really do anything you don't choose to do of your own free will."

"You mean I have to do it myself?"

"Now you are talking reality."

"Will you be there to help me?"

"I will give you whatever support I can, but the transformative process is one you go through yourself. Somehow you have to really believe that healing is possible, that a healing force will be there when you need it as you let go of your defense system."

"What have I got to lose? I am unhappy with my life the way it is."

"You make your own choices. As you let go of defensiveness and the need to control everything, you need to keep a constant awareness and readiness to make choices in any situation, no matter how difficult the things are which come up."

"Can I think about it?"

"I don't know how to answer that. You are the only one making choices about your own life." End of conversation.

We fool no one, not even ourselves, about our ability to change. Hanging on to a sinking ship may seem safer because it is known. But setting out and swimming, sailing, letting go to new life can open a whole fresh world if we would but risk enough to enter it. Who knows what there might be when we let go of the old worn out ship of our lives. A new one waiting for us just beyond the next wave? You will never know until you risk.

When is the time ripe for you?

Transformation means complete change, a change which leads to greater meaning and wholeness in one's life, but it does not usually happen all at once, totally, in an instant. So we can now relax and deal with our natural fear of change.

Enter The Archetypes

As you can see from the following drawing of The Seven Basic Archetypes, certain primaries of the universe, and in life itself, can be recognized in this model of the archetypes.

At the center is **the Central Archetype of the Self**, the integrative, differentiating and transforming archetype of unity.

And around this central archetype are the primary pairs of opposites which relate to each other through contrariety and the creating of new unities.

The **Masculine** of thrusting, assertiveness, and directed focus toward a goal, comes together in unity with the **Feminine,** the archetype of encompassment, flow, and nurturing, at the locus of the Self. The product of their union is the new possibility symbolized by the **Divine Child,** one manifestation of the Self, celebrated on such holidays as Christmas and summer solstice, and even on our own birthdays.

Then we have another great pair of archetypal opposites, the **Heroic** and **Adversity**, or Hero-Heroine and Adversary. In all the epics and novels these archetypes play themselves out, as they also do in our own lives. Suffice it to say here that our personal egos tend to side with the Heroic, the good, the just, the savior, and reject the Adversary, the bad, evil, that which opposes and destroys in life.

The **persona**, or good side of ourselves which we show to the world, is usually built out of the qualities of the Heroic and either the Masculine or Feminine archetypes with which we are sexually identified.

The **shadow**, our more hidden, underdeveloped and rejected side which comes out most in intimate relationships, is made up of elements from the Adversary archetype and from the opposite of the Masculine or Feminine with which we are identified.

Typically, my shadow as a man will be opposing, power hungry, manipulative, tricky, irrational, peculiar, crazy, visionary, etc., that strange mix created of unconscious unity between my Feminine and Adversary archetypes. My persona as a man, on the other hand, may be assertive, helpful, effective, understanding, successful and knowledgeable.

The woman's persona might be relational, warm, inspired, ecstatic, devoted to beauty and healing, flowing and accepting, wise and protective. Her shadow derives its qualities from the Masculine and Adversary archetypes and shows itself as bitchy, irrational or too rational, domineering, manipulative, raging, compulsively overproductive, and so on.

The last great pair of primary archetypes are **Journey** and **Death-Rebirth**, embodied especially in the stages of life. Behind the Journey archetype is the urge to grow and develop, and to seek a direction for one's life. The Death-Rebirth archetype, on the other hand, asserts itself in transition periods such as births, marriages, and deaths.

The Ego and The Seven Basic Archetypes

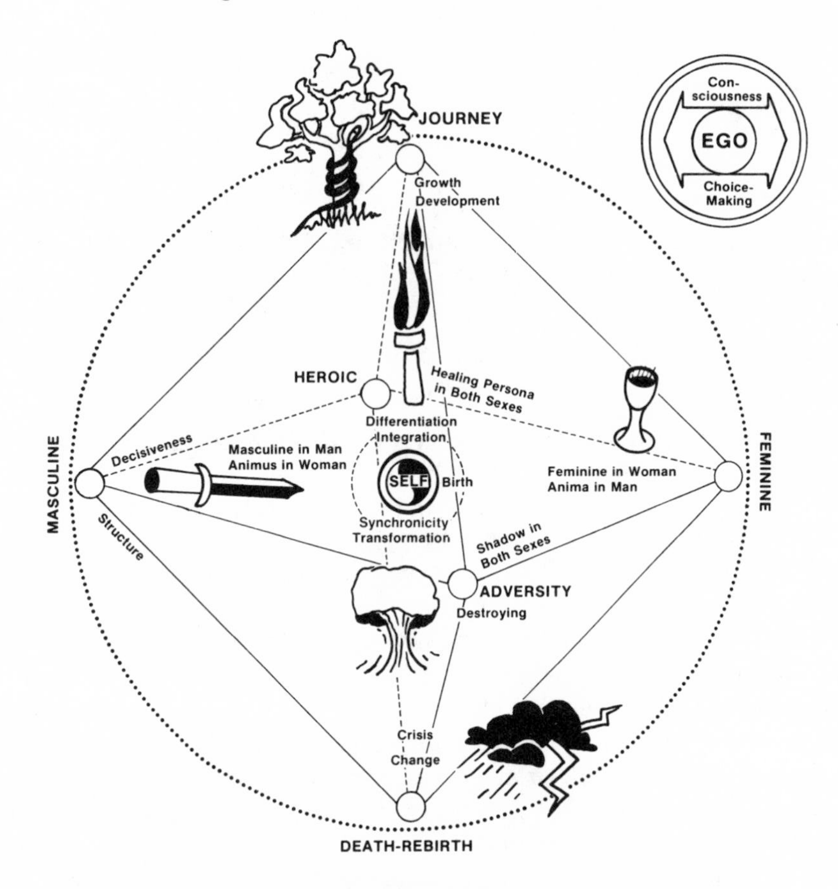

This diagram shows the major dynamics of the psyche and life, called archetypes or innate energy forms. They are interrelated through the laws of opposites. If we become identified with one archetypal energy this will cause the opposite archetypal energy to come up, often in intense form. The ego diagram shows the essential functions for relating to archetypal life energy.

What Are Life Principles?

The universe rests on principles, the innate laws of the interrelations between things.

Life, indeed all existence, would not hold together for an instant unless there were innate ways or principles that structured how things work.

Archetypes are the innate energy clusters or innate essences of the universe, and their principles or laws govern the ways they interrelate to form life and existence itself.
I am a being who exists according to the innate principles of the universe.
I live because the universe wants life in me.

Do these affirmations excite you? We talked earlier of how we all have images of ourselves, such as man, woman, child, etc., which we use to define ourselves. Now we are looking at a deeper level of things so that we can begin to understand ourselves and operate more effectively and meaningfully in the world.

I have within me opposites which need integration and consciousness within and without.

Throughout this book we will be suggesting principles, affirmations and intentions about how life really works. Practicing these principles is a way of becoming realistic about life and aiding in your own and others' fulfillment. You have nothing and everything to lose if you do not make yourself conscious to yourself. You are already working on your own consciousness and seeking life change. Whenever you talk about yourself and your life you are seeking consciousness. Whenever you read a meaningful book or attend a workshop you are seeking change and development in your life. What is added here is what you already know deep in your intuitive self. We are making things clearer as we work together. We include principles as teachings throughout this book and we include exercises for experiencing the principles articulated here. Everything is in your hands. Everything is love. Everything happens now.

Principles To Live By

In creating practical applications of the material in this book it will be helpful to keep the following basic principles in mind.

1. We are not what we seem.

2. Who I am determines how I live life.

3. Archetypes are the innate energies of the universe. It is through their dynamics that we and all creatures and objects have being.

4. We project what has not been made conscious. Projection is putting out there what is really inside ourselves. We need to project, we need to see something as out there before we can experience it as within, but we also need to continually take back our projections to achieve our own wholeness.

5. Wholeness is the major goal in life for self-realizing persons. To continually become whole we must express and integrate all sides of ourselves, not just what we call the good or better side. We must bring into unity all the major opposites of our being. This is a life-work and a daily practice which can lead one to realizing the purpose and destiny for one's life.

6. We are not simply males and females. We are persons. This means that to realize our true identity we must develop within ourselves both the masculine and feminine, as well as other archetypal energies.

7. Falling in love is a projection experience which proves the archetypes exist. We identify with one archetype and project the other and then seek experiences of unity, as in sex, to get the projected part of ourselves back again. If I do not eventually learn to take back the love projection I will hurt my ability to relate to others and to integrate the opposites within myself.

8. Sex is one major expression of the archetype of unity, the Self, the most central archetype of all existence. The archetype of unity is what brings the opposites together to create new life and is that which harmonizes and continually re-creates the world, as well as our individual being.

9. The goal of life is wholeness and the way to that goal is the practice of bringing resolution to all conflicts. To do this we must give up old and inadequate ways of dealing with conflicts and develop that which is

most meaningful and truly works. Personal transformation occurs when I practice achieving wholeness through integration and bringing resolution to conflicts.

10. Sickness is a part of myself being at odds with other parts of myself. Healing is bringing resolution to conflicts by including the opposites.

11. We are all in need of healing every day whether we have a physical illness or not. The equivalent of physical sickness in the psychological and spiritual sphere is conflict. Conflict occurs when we become one-sided and therefore in opposition to another side within or without.

12. Healing involves both sacrifice and bringing resolution. Sacrifice is needed as a choice to let go of that which is outdated and strangles new life. Resolution means resolving conflicts between opposites by creating new unities out of them. Transformation occurs out of the process of bringing resolution to each successive conflict.

13. We resist healing and sacrifice because we have attitudes which tell us, what is mine belongs to me forever, or, what I have now is better than what I can obtain in the future. We can choose to let go of these life-suffocating attitudes and adopt new ones based on realistic spiritual principles.

14. The way to life is to let go of the past to be fully present in the present so the future can be born.

15. The enemy is within. Most people live and die immersed in more conflicts than they ever resolve. We tend not to really resolve conflicts but to repress them or hide them from ourselves by identifying with one opposite and repressing and projecting the other. What we identify with we call good. What we reject and repress we call bad.

16. A personal goal I can choose now for my life is in this self-affirmation that, **I am more and more able to experience the natural conflicts in my life and to bring them to resolution.** This is a major step for the courageous, those who know their own fears but move onward anyway.

17. Trying to overcome power with power is no way to resolve conflicts. Even if you defeat and annihilate your enemy, or an opposite within yourself, the conditions for the conflict remain and will surface

again, this time probably in an even more extreme form. What I try to leave behind meets me at the next gate.

18. Repression as well as identification causes projection. Repression causes projection of the shadow, the rejected parts of ourselves. This leads to defensiveness and a lack of true resolution of conflicts.

19. I am the opposite I project. I am not only what I identify with and see as myself.

20. I seek to clarify and resolve all issues and conflicts in my life as they come up. This is an intention to which I can commit myself in order to live a transforming life. What I do not resolve I must necessarily repress. It takes energy to repress energy and therefore the more I repress the less energy I will have for living life fully.

21. Resolving issues in life is a daily practice based on making choices which sacrifice the unnecessary and create new unities out of the opposites in the situation or in myself.

22. Principles are formulations of the innate laws about how life really works. I am a being who exists according to the innate principles of the universe. I can choose to make conscious those principles and live them fully in my life.

THIS DAY I CHOOSE TO BEGIN RESOLVING THE CONFLICTS BETWEEN OPPOSITES IN MY LIFE.

PART III

THE CREATIVE EGO

Evolution

Many thousands and thousands of years ago there was a great evolutionary step, maybe as great as any that has ever happened.

Picture our ancestors somewhere, in a swamp or forest, feeling identified with all things, one's group, the sun and moon, the animals, the total environment. Back then everything was considered One and Paradise. We were all part of everyone else. We had sex but did not know it caused babies to grow in the womb. We had anger and love but did not know that we could do anything about these great emotions. We saw the world as God, one Universal Whole, but did not see ourselves as separate beings.

We did not have choice.

We had no objectivity.

Then one day back before recorded time someone, maybe a child, gave more than a grunt. The child asked a question and with that question consciousness was born. The child did not follow blind instinct but asked the first question and was hit for it, yelling and screaming, but did not give up her question. This was a formulation which changed everything, for to ask questions we must place in doubt and ignorance everything which is. We must question what we see, doubt what we think, and wonder over what we feel. We must recognize ourselves as objects of our own emotions and want to know how we as individuals are different and separate from everything else.

As a simple exercise, recall for a moment your earliest childhood experience of choice, or of conscious awareness of yourself as a separate and unique being in the universe. What were your feelings and reactions then? Did you have questions? Were you forced into making an important life choice? Were you isolated from others by your experience?

So within each individual life from childhood on upward we replay the whole evolutionary history of what it is to have become human.

This process includes the birth of the ego.

The Ego As Choice-Maker

The ego is that conscious part of ourselves which makes choices and serves as the focus of consciousness of who we are and what we are doing.

The ego is the choice-making and consciousness-carrying function of the personality. It is that which directs the energy available to it, and that which helps organize and then makes sense out of all the perceptions which arise. The ego activates the memory banks to access the desired information for making choices. The ego also has many images of itself which it identifies with. I am a mother, father, student, etc. These identities are all ego functions and necessary for the full development of personality, but the ego is not the whole of the personality. Far from it.

I am not who I think I am.

I am more than I am consciously aware of.

The ego is also a whole set of attitudes about life, and about itself, which it uses in making its own choices.

Attitudes are usually unconscious contents out of which we choose. If I have an underlying belief or attitude that I am more and more effective in my life, then chances are I will make choices which actualize more and more of life's potentials.

I choose what I become.

If I see myself as inadequate and see the world as out to get me, then I will make choices which create inadequacy and fear of the future.

I can more and more decide how I choose in life.

My ego is the choice-making and consciousness-carrying function of myself. I affirm these functions as keys to my own wholeness. I will work not to stay identified with any one side or opposite within myself so that I may equally relate to all opposites as needed.

When is the time to make choices which affirm softness and flow in my life?

When is the time to choose firmness and decisiveness in a situation?

The ego makes choices regarding what to evoke and affirm in each moment. This is the creative ego function even though most of us choose inadequately sometimes.

Why Do We Sometimes Choose Inadequacy?

Choice is always a choice. We do not have to become conscious. Even when we are desperate we can choose to die instead of change and realize ourselves.

The ego limits itself when,

* It tries to choose only for itself in every situation,
* It identifies with certain roles and life energies to the exclusion of others,
* It tries to avoid choice by drifting with the tides,
* It chooses to react to circumstances instead of enact circumstances with preparation and consciousness,
* It will not commit itself to anything but itself and its own point of view.

The Necessity for Commitment

Most of us make commitments in our lives as a way of getting involved and going deep with an activity.

Commitment is sustained choice over a specific period of time.

We do not always like our commitments but we make them because we know that living without commitments can keep us at the surface of things.

Marriage is different from simply living intimately together because in marriage there is a given commitment to stay together through the ups and downs of the relationship, no matter what. This is why once married always married, even if the relationship ends up in death or divorce.

Our spouses live deeply within us long after we may have ceased relating to them in the outer. This is an example of how far a commitment can take one in life.

The creative ego needs to strengthen itself to become more and more effective, and practicing commitment is one way to do this.

The Regressive Pull

It is so easy for any of us to make a choice and then seek to change it when negative consequences start coming in. **We love only the positive consequences of our choices and seek to flee from or neglect the negative consequences.**

This is also called the **regressive pull**. When we finally make a new choice, which means sacrificing the old as well as choosing for new life, we may still want to back out of it, especially if things become hard. I have known a number of men who experience feelings of wanting to back out of a marriage, not just before the ceremony, if then, but when their wives are pregnant and close to giving birth. They unconsciously fear the next step, the real marriage, which is being bonded to that particular woman for a long time because of their mutual responsibility in bringing up the child. The lesson is, be wary of having a child if you do not both want it.

And when young, know what you are doing if you marry or live with someone who does not want to have children with you. The regressive pull says in a secret little voice, "Don't move on, don't take the next more responsible step in life. You're not ready for it yet. Play around some more. Have a good time first."

We are never ready for the next step in life. We take the plunge to challenge and make ourselves adequate to the potentials and tasks ahead.

Once we have made a commitment we open the door to the new, and to a trap door which would collapse under us, sucking our choices into unconscious withdrawal. We become sleepy, lazy, ineffective. We seek pleasure, trying to crawl back into the lap of the Great Mother of contentment and peace, instead of struggling and breaking through.

We make commitments in order to call up the Adversary consciously so that we may do battle. Sometimes it is important to wait until a boat drifts by to take us to the farther shore. But much of our lives we must plunge in, cutting against the current, giving our all to the encounter, to make it to the next destination in our lives.

We fear the future. We love the pleasure of feeling warm and secure. We don't like to suffer. We even find friends who say take it easy, don't work so hard, have fun in life, right when we need to make that extra push if we are to break through to fresh being.

There are a thousand ways to say "No" and only one way to say "Yes" to life. What we choose is what we become.

Dealing Creatively With Consequences

You consider the alternatives, allow the tension between opposites to build, and when the moment is ripe choose that which most resolves the conflict and creates a sense of new wholeness for you. This is the process of creative choice-making, but then we move on to the next step which is the dealing with the outcomes.

Outcomes or consequences are the natural result of our actions. They are neither good nor bad. They just are and it is their reality with which we must deal if we are to realize the full potentials of our choices.

I make my choices and I choose also to actively deal with the consequences of my choices.

Let me suggest that it takes a full commitment to life to actively make choices and deal with the outcomes thereof.

Things will rarely go the way we expect them to in life. To expect the unexpected is reality.

I have freedom only in my choices. I do not have freedom to determine the outcomes which result.

I do have freedom in how I deal with the outcomes of my choices.

Most things can only be known after the choice is made, not before.

A true commitment is one which not only chooses between alternatives but which also chooses to deal with the outcome no matter what results.

There is a certain kind and depth of knowledge which only comes after the commitment, and not before it. So why not choose to act when the moment is ripe and deal with what results?

Themes in Review

1. **How I choose is what I become.** My ego is the choice-making and consciousness-carrying function in myself. This is the creative ego which I need in order to develop effectiveness in life.

2. We sometimes choose inadequacy in life because we are caught in ego limitations such as choosing only for oneself or not committing oneself to anything of value.

3. **Commitment is sustained choice over a definite period of time.** The deepest knowledge can only be learned through making a commitment to a life process. Commitment is the secret to effectiveness.

4. A natural part of every choice is dealing with the regressive pull, that which would draw us back into past ways, past values, or inactivity.

5. I make my choices and I also choose to deal with the consequences. I have freedom only in what I choose, not in the outcomes of my choices. **Most things can only be known after the choice is made.**

The Attitudes Which Rule Our Lives

There is an army of dictators within each of us which dictate and rule our lives. Most of the time we do not know who these dictators are. We only feel their presence in each action and thought. We especially feel something is wrong when we become angry or frustrated about something that has happened to us.

Most of us get terribly upset over the little things, such as a scratch on the furniture or a meal which doesn't taste so good. Or if these kinds of things do not upset you, how about when someone offers you criticism, whether justified or not?

* What if someone calls you up at the wrong moment?
* What if you just found out that the repair of your car will cost hundreds of dollars?
* What if the doctor calls and invites you down to his office to tell you you have cancer?
* What if you receive a new promotion and cannot sleep that night out of fear of the added responsibility?
* What if your anger is making life difficult for you?
* What if your love partner informs you one bright sunny day that he or she no longer wants to relate to you?
* What if you are having a hard time finding the right place to live?
* What if you are restless and have a hard time sleeping at night?

* What if you want to have a child and can't seem to conceive?
* What if you don't really know what to do with your life?
* What if you are feeling continually defeated by your compulsions, whether over-eating, over-sleeping, smoking, over-working or darker sexual compulsions. What then?
* What if you are scared about dying?
* What if you want to fulfill yourself in life but don't know where to turn for the right guidance?

By now, if you are sensitive, you may be a bit upset over having read the above list of "what ifs", but don't shy away. This is life, life in the raw, life lived inadequately because we are in the grip of unconscious patterns and attitudes. **I can almost promise you that if you really look at how attitudes work inside yourself and in your choice-making you can live a changed life.**

Making conscious and changing the attitudes which unconsciously control us leads to a transformed life.

We must get at those hidden dictators which control our behavior, and sacrifice as many as we can find into the fires of transformation.

Let us strike a bargain, you and I. I will be as clear as possible in helping you change your attitudes towards life, and you in turn will choose to change one attitude a month in yourself for as long as you can last, or as long as is necessary for your own wholeness.

Think of it. One attitude a month changed towards wholeness and reality equals twelve in one year. You will begin to be rich in life and not just have more money in your bank account, though this could also result.

The Process for Changing Attitudes

Attitudes are the unconscious contexts out of which we make our choices. We can make these attitudes conscious, change them through working with affirmations and intentions, and make new more vital choices using life principles which we take as our new contexts for choice-making.

First, look at the previous list of "what ifs," choose one and see what it evokes for you.

I will now choose one myself and work with it.

* What if I find out that the repair of my car will cost hundreds of dollars?

Good. My first reaction is fear, fear that I don't have enough money to cover the repairs. My second reaction is anger, anger that life is dealing me this blow which I do not deserve. I have kept my car in good shape. My third reaction is hurt that I won't be able to spend the money on something which could give me pleasure, pleasure in good food or several nights of good entertainment. I feel depressed by this intrusion on my reality.

But wait a minute. These are all reactions. Who says I have to act this way? Maybe my mother's attitude about how hard it is to get money is making me afraid? Maybe an attitude I got from an idealistic teacher is telling me that "money doesn't matter anyway" and I have not been careful enough with my income over the past year to allow for serious expenses? Maybe also I am being unduly influenced by an attitude I have that life is being really good to me right now and so when something goes against me I get angry and upset?

Once I bring an attitude to consciousness I can choose to let go of it and face the situation consciously. **I always have choice in how I ultimately react to things.**

Right here in my new behavior I am substituting life principles for unconscious attitudes. They are,

* **I always have choice in how I deal with situations.**

* **I can choose and re-choose to let go of automatic ways of reacting to life events after making them conscious.**

* **Bringing consciousness to a situation makes us more effective in dealing with it.**

* **There is always a creative solution to every problem in life.**

In working with my car repair example I have found out what my unconscious attitudes are, sacrificed them, and chosen more real and purposeful attitudes to put in their place. I have now opened myself to the best solution, not the worst, in the circumstances. Who knows? I might even sell the car and get another one more appropriate to my present stage in life.

Some New Creative Attitudes

Life principles can also be used as affirmations. Affirmations are declarations which change reality-denying attitudes into reality-affirming statements based on principles of how we and life really work.

My new attitudes in dealing with my car repair and other challenges shall be,

* I will start allowing 20% of my time, energy and money to go towards accepting and dealing with waste and adversity.
* I don't always have to get my way in life in order to be fulfilled.
* I am capable of earning the money I need in life to sustain myself.
* My goal in life is wholeness, not pleasure and well-being.

I am also dealing with the problem by creating intentions for myself, acts I will carry out in resolving the situation.

* I choose to make conscious the attitudes behind my immediate reactions.
* I choose to let go of or sever myself from life-defeating attitudes which were evoked.
* I choose to take action to change my situation for the better so that the next time a similar circumstance happens I will be consciously prepared for it.

This is how the process works. To test it for yourself you can take a "what if?" or actual situation from your own life and apply the procedure.

I can use every outer event, positive or negative, as an inner opportunity to create change.

And it works superbly. We not only greatly change ourselves, but usually change outer circumstances towards more fullness and wholeness.

Using Affirmations and Intentions to Change Attitudes

Embedded in the above process is a basic procedure for changing oneself which is being further developed throughout this book. In the practices section later on you will encounter specific practices on how to find your attitudes and change them using principles, affirmations and intentions.

This approach differs significantly from other approaches to using affirmations or positive intentions. We are not interested in your making a million dollars or finding the perfect mate. Our focus is change through developing a perspective on oneself which works in reality. We offer not "pie in the sky" philosophy, or talk about "perfect peace" and "perfect love." We offer no fantasies or delusions about reality. You accept in this approach both the positive and negative and you learn how to deal with both. You do not escape one by going into the other.

An affirmation as the "positivists" describe it is a positive statement which idealistically asks the reader to exclude the negative opposite, thereby creating endless guilt and inadequacy in the heart of the practitioner. Have you ever tried to work with the following from *A Course in Miracles* and its popularizing book, *Love Is Letting Go of Fear*?

"This day I choose to spend in perfect peace."

Ah bliss! My wife has just left me but everything's wonderful. I have perfect peace. All I had to do was choose it. The stock market just crashed and the death squads have killed and mutilated thirty more victims in a small country in Central America. I saw the pictures in a weekly magazine but I choose perfect peace today. I'm safe in America and nothing can get through to me.

Do we make a point? Here is another positive statement from the same approach. "The past is over—it can touch me not."

How wonderful! All my patterns built up in childhood don't touch me anymore. I'm new! I'm pure! But why do I still feel hurt sometimes when I don't get what I want? Is something wrong with me? Am I just repressing my past instead of dealing with it? Are these "miracle people" right or are they trying to put something over on me? They tell me I can't love if I have fear. Yet I'm afraid when I love because it's such a powerful emotion when I let myself feel it fully.

Therapists with integrity go through the roof when they hear the New Age Popularizers telling everyone that their problems are all due to not being positive enough. I recently saw a well-known psychic give a whole line of people asking questions of her this "sweet mother's milk" and never once suggest that there were good therapists available who could help them work on their problems. The people in line to ask questions recited woe after woe from their personal lives and the best she could do was give them back popular spiritual psychology. Just change your attitude to a positive one and everything will be all right. You don't have to deal with the negative. You don't have to get into fear. You can switch to love.

What a contrast this new religion of pop psychology is to the in-depth work which goes on behind the scenes in the offices of professional therapists. Therapists who work in private know what real suffering is like. They miss the limelight that the misleading gurus obtain, but they are the ones doing the healing journey with people.

The affirmations and life principles offered here are designed to reflect fundamental aspects of reality. They are believable because they include the opposites. They often have practices associated with them. They are not presented in perfect or one-sided terms and so do not evoke the kind of negativity and inadequacy that extremisms evoke. In place of "Love is the absence of fear" substitute "Love is the acceptance which makes possible the dealing with fear." Watch carefully how these issues are dealt with in this book. We plunge ahead.

Love is the acceptance which makes possible the dealing with fear.

Image Identifications which Limit Our Reality

I am not who I think I am. I am always changing.

We remember that one thing all egos tend to do is identify with roles and images based on archetypes.

In adolescence most people strongly identify with their biological sex. This is the archetypal movement most prevalent at that time. The boy becomes a man and the girl becomes a woman. It will be time for them to leave their original families and form new families of their own.

Each will identify with one opposite, project the other one onto a lover, and mate with him or her to re-contact and experience the projected energy.

The ego in this process becomes thoroughly identified with either masculine or feminine.

What happens when the male and female roles in society break down as is happening today? Some strong identifications usually still occur but a lot more choice-making will have to come into play because the participants in this drama are not always sure who they are or what they are supposed to do. Who does the dishes? Who changes the diapers? Who does the cooking? Who goes out and gets a full time job to support the family? Who initiates love-making? Who is on top in sex? Who pays the bills? Who makes choices about what to do tonight?

The list is endless and varied. In the old days couples were supposed to totally accept cultural and archetypal roles. This created strong identifications and lessened the need to make choices. Each had his or her roles and responsibilities in the life process. Ah! The old days when everything was simple and clear and unconscious.

Who Am I?

* I am a man. I am a woman. I am a person.

* I am hungry. For the moment I am identified with my stomach. If my stomach is large I am compulsively identified with it.

* I am a mother. I am a father. I am a child.

* I am a good person. I am an unhappy person.

* I am a doctor. I am a nurse. You are the patient.

* I am a white, middle class American. I am Black. I am Chicano. I am an Englishman. I am a worker. I am a beer drinker.

Again, the list is endless and easily proves its point. We have a tendency to identify with all sorts of images for ourselves instead of relating to them as functions, as ways of acting in certain situations.

The Way Through

Most of us want to have an interesting and varied life. We do not want to become stuck in a role forever. The danger in identifying with a certain image or role is that this limits us from acting in other, even contrary ways. Why can't a man be warm and flowing with his children sometimes and the woman be decisive and authoritative?

The answer, the possibility, is that we can do both. **We can disidentify from one archetypal opposite in order to relate to both.**

"You take out the garbage tonight. I'm sick of playing the house cleaner."

"All right, I will, but then you cook. I want a vacation from the mother archetype."

And so it goes in a creative relationship in which both partners are working on their own and each other's wholeness.

Couples may still differentiate and take certain roles and activities as each person's own. This must also happen as the rule of nature. But we can still choose to intervene and change situations from time to time to create renewal and to play with life's energies.

Who wants to be an old stick-in-the-mud and not continually try new things? Life is so rich! Can anyone really choose to be that dead to the world?

Summary

1. There is a secret army of dictators within each of us. This is the army of largely unconscious attitudes which tend to rule our lives.

2. Attitudes are the unconscious contexts out of which we make our choices. We can choose to find out about these attitudes and substitute for the unrealistic ones new life principles on which to base our lives.

3. We change attitudes by bringing them to consciousness and then using affirmations and intentions and adopting new life principles for living our lives. Affirmations are creative changes in attitude. Intentions are commitments to specific actions embodying new attitudes and life principles.

4. We can choose to use every outer life event as a possibility for inner change.

5. **I am not what I think I am. I am always changing.** The ego identifies with certain images for itself. But any image identifications, however necessary, become limiting and anti-life in the long run.

6. We disidentify from archetypal images and patterns through sacrificing the identification and consciously evoking the opposite of the identification.

PART IV
EGOCENTRICITIES AND HOW TO TRANSFORM THEM

Egocentricities

The human creature is sometimes a wonderful being. Think on it. Do you like yourself and others? Do you feel you are wonderful sometimes?

This could be a sign of healthy growth.**I am a being rich in resources with a deep love of life.**

Say this affirmation a number of times to yourself and see how you feel about it.

Chances are it will make you uncomfortable. I hate to say it but most of us have to struggle to truly affirm ourselves.

But what is the reality? Am I all that special a person?

You could be, but you would have to make conscious your abilities, your innate destiny and dignity, and live them fully. **What stands in the way?**

Feelings and images of inferiority and self-doubt?

Personality patterns resulting from childhood denial and trauma?

Again we emphasize **the way of healing is a way of transformation, a way of letting go of the old and actualizing the new.**

What stands in the way?

Our egocentricities stand in the way! To be egocentric is to be so totally focused on oneself and one's needs that nothing else matters.

Either we are egocentric by feeling inferior and acting inadequate to life, all the while secretly judging others and ourselves for not being more perfect, or we go to the other extreme and see ourselves as superior to everyone else and seek to show this by controlling situations for our own benefit, while underneath feeling inferior and being also the laughing butt for those around us.

The Egocentricity of Acting Better Than Anyone Else

I don't really care to live my life in considerations of how others will judge me. I have one life to live and it shall be my own.

How does this affirmation or attitude strike you? Is this a value you would want to achieve in your life?

I do care about others who matter to me or influence my life. But still I must live as if I matter most to the healing process, the life journey to which I am committed.

This last affirmation is one I can move with personally. I do not live in a vacuum but within interrelations, yet still I must make my own choices, influenced more by the source of new life.

The egocentric ego is one which tries to keep center stage and is at the same time compulsively susceptible underneath to others' demands and expectations. Picture someone you know who is often trying to be the center of attention, trying even harder when no one laughs at his jokes or appreciates her stories.

Be quiet and listen. Listen to yourself. Listen to the still, warm heart inside. It will tell you the way. It will say to you that it is all right to be exactly who you are and not have to meet anyone else's images or expectations.

In social or work situations just relax and let things be. Destroy the compulsion to do. Be ready to participate, but you do not have to compete or strive to be heard and affirmed by others or yourself.

I am my own person. I am all right the way I am.

I am flowing and open to the needs of reality.

I am one who follows the inward journey. I do not have to force anyone to like me or do what I want.

The Egocentricity of Inadequacy

Most of us, if we are not dominators, are surely victims. We go around in life practicing inadequacy because at heart we are really afraid to succeed and use our resources to the fullest.

A victim type is a dependent person often acting out feelings and ego-images of inferiority to get others to help him or her do things which are best done by oneself.

A perfect egocentric friendship, or wedding, is one in which a dominator gets together with a self-denying person. They will prey on each other, each in their own way.

One person will always be demonstrating the need for help, yet will never do anything right in the other person's eyes. The dominator will feel both important and frustrated at being able to tell someone else what to do, even though nothing ever really gets done right, whatever right is.

Don't laugh. Do laugh, but recognize that these characteristics are in you and me—are they not?—and are part of the human condition.

I will accept my foibles so that they do not dominate me.

This too is one of the important principles of healing. **We must first accept the compulsion we are in before we can transform it. We must often live it fully before we can become released from it.** We must live our automatic tendencies in creative ways which put them to work.

We all get angry and fearful about ourselves. The goal is not to get rid of these natural emotions, but to use them creatively as part of the journey.

You do not get over fear by living only love. You deal with fear by accepting and experiencing it fully. The "living only love" people would have you simply drop your fear and rage, something like dropping your pants, I guess, and going around half naked. If we are going to wear clothes, we need the whole outfit, not just certain parts.

You cannot love your neighbor as yourself unless you can experience fully your own self-hate. If you accept and deal with your own self-hate you will not project fear and hatred out onto others.

"So I hate myself from time to time, leave me alone. Don't try to make me be good all the time. If I scare you when I get dark, that's your problem. Let me deal with my feelings and you deal with yours."

I will experience fully all my feelings, including my self-hatred, and transform them constructively.

Self-hatred can become self-evaluation, can become passion for new life. Self-criticalness can help cure inflation and innocence.

Fear can become the touchstone for sensing danger to oneself and others and doing what is necessary to protect the values and dynamics involved.

Love is not the absence of fear.
Love is not the absence of hatred.
Love is the embracing of each aspect of life to transform it by integrating it within the whole.

Love does not deny violence but seeks to transform it.
Love does not deny fear but seeks to transform it.
Love does not deny hatred but seeks to transform it.
The partners to all our thoughts and actions are their opposites.

We cannot escape the opposites in life. We can only choose to accept and deal with them through differentiation and integration. Before we can integrate, or take within our being, we must differentiate. We learn to separate out the different parts of ourselves. We also learn to separate experiences and projections into what is mine and what is yours, so that we can become clear. The essence of struggle, as many couples find out, is to separate out what belongs where. Struggle brings out genuine as well as exaggerated differences. It is important to place differences in appropriate relation to each other as well as to integrate and unify them into one whole.

Drink the bitter and the sweet in life and you have fullness.

The Egocentricity of Self-Will

Maybe the greatest egocentricity of them all is self-will, the belief that I can govern and change my thoughts simply through choice and will-power.

Think positively and positive things will happen for you in your life.

Think negatively and negative things will happen to you in your life.

But this view of controlling one's thoughts does not include the opposites, and therein lies the fatal flaw. We must include both the positive and negative in life to achieve wholeness.

I have worked with and seen many people in my practice who come in to a therapy hour complaining of life's frustrations and how difficult it is to cope with them. They have tried will-power, positive thinking, this growth teaching and that, all sorts of spiritual practices, and still they feel like they are not realizing themselves.

They come to me and the first thing we do is work on acceptance.

What's wrong with that? Why do you have to change that? What is the hurry? What is so terrible about that? Are you sure it is all really that bad? What is it you most fear about yourself?

The next thing we may do is experience together what they have been fighting. The egocentricity of self-will creates resistance to change. Denying one opposite, one side of life, creates resistance to the opposite you are trying to live.

If you would love, accept hate and anger within yourself.

If you would be conscious, accept your ongoing ability to blank out on important things in your life.

I forget what I'm supposed to remember about blanking out.

If you would be effective, accept inadequacy, accept that you will always fail at things, your life being a trail of error as well as accomplishment.

Because we are imperfect we would be perfect. **Which is better, to strive for perfection, or accept inadequacy?**

In this approach healing comes through wholeness and individuation, not self-will. We accept the opposites within ourselves and in life and work for their integration.

The stronger the real ego as choice-maker is, the less egocentric it will need to be.

Themes In Summary

1. **I am a being rich in resources with a deep love of life.** Therefore I do not have to live egocentrically, choosing just for myself alone.

2. I show my egocentricity by acting or trying to be better than others and by trying to control and dominate situations. Behind such a tendency are usually feelings of inferiority and of not having found one's life purpose.

3. I am my own person. I am all right the way I am. I am one who follows the inward journey. I do not have to force anyone to like me or do what I want.

4. The egocentricity of inadequacy is one in which I play victim to myself and others. I choose to stay inadequate and afraid of life's fullness which can be mine.

5. You do not get over fear by living only love. You deal with fear by experiencing it fully. It is not fear we have to fear, but our identification with it. We can choose to experience fear and use it as a signal to creatively protect ourselves in the face of a one-sided and therefore life-denying experience. If we go to the one side in anything we will fear the other side coming up. If I plunge completely into a love experience I will fear its ending. If, however, I practice daily disidentifying from it, I will be creatively protecting myself from its power. I will also be more able to integrate what it evokes.

6. Love is not the absence of fear, hate or other real and dark emotions necessary to life. **Love is that process which affirms and accepts all the opposites so that they may be made conscious and transformed within the integrative life. Only that love is real which leads to the unity of opposites.**

7. Maybe the greatest egocentricity of them all is self-will, the assumption and choice that I as ego can choose my reality simply through choice and power. **The ego is not the center of the universe and never will be.**

8. **We deal with our egocentricities by making them conscious and getting to the hurt, woundedness and sense of inferiority behind them.** The egocentric ego will always feel inferior no matter what it chooses or accomplishes unless it makes the One Choice to let go of focusing on itself, and instead serve a larger, more inclusive process than it will ever be.

The Creative Ego Chooses For Reality

We hope you have realized by now that this is not a course for dissolving ego. Dealing with egocentricity, yes. Getting rid of or diminishing ego, no.

The development of the ego-function within the human personality was one of the great evolutionary steps and must be preserved at all costs, and despite what certain religions may tell us. In fact, **the stronger the real ego is, the less egocentric or self-centered it will need to be.**

The evolutionary moment of asking the first question, that first point of consciousness, rings in our ears and hearts.

The question in itself is the blow to all dogma, all belief systems including this one.

We need stronger and stronger egos to deal with life more and more fully. We are not interested in dogma or absolute belief, the refuge of the frail and halting ego. We are interested in the risk-taking ego continually questioning and open to new ideas.

We are putting out the best information and life principles we know, coming from personal and community experience and the traditions of the ages. But whatever is said here must be questioned, tested, acted upon, for consciousness to occur.

We are as much interested in practices as in ideas. If you have methods which lead to experience, you do not need dogmas. If you have only experience, however, and no way of making it conscious, of developing concepts out of it, then you have life but no perspective on life. And where will that lead you?

The Eternal
What is Life?
Purpose?
Destiny
SKW

PART V

PRACTICES FOR PERSONAL TRANSFORMATION

Creating Change in Your Life

I once was conducting a workshop presenting what I thought was important material. It was good material and people were taking to it, but all of a sudden a number of participants were not satisfied. They expressed a need to change and did not know how to go about it.

Immediately my alternatives became either to continue with my good material or to switch to their area of concern and modify my workshop format.

I chose to change and in the next session presented new material on how to create change in your own life. What followed was one of the most exciting and revelatory two hours of my life. Join me now as we go through a similar process. You may question what you are being asked to do, but you can make the commitment to go ahead anyway.

Attitudes Against Change

Most egos resist change. The ego likes being comfortable in the known, in what it has already worked so hard to establish. Some attitudes of resistance to change are,

* It won't work anyway, it never does.
* I don't think I should have to suffer in order to change.
* I don't need anyone's help to change.
* I'm so inadequate that I'll never be able to change.

These are attitudes and not absolutes. You can choose to do away with ones like these which affect yourself. And as always, substitute new principles and affirmations for the old.

* I can choose change in my life every day.
* I am more and more capable of changing things in my life.
* I can change my attitude about what is happening to me.
* If I want something I may get it, although not necessarily in the form I expected.

What for you would be creative change attitudes? Write out some now for yourself.

1.

2.

3.

4.

5.

6.

What Do I Most Need to Change in My Life Right Now?

We all need to change in life. Reality is always shifting and we always have new problems and potentials to deal with.

How I deal with problems is a crucial issue behind whether I lead a fulfilling life or not.

Why not list one to three major things about yourself you need to change right now. Be specific. List them as goals, focusing on the new possibility as well as on what blocks you from realizing it.

1.

2.

3.

Someone in a workshop mentioned that her only problem was procrastination. This would be focusing only on what blocks her. When she worked further, and saw the transforming side, she discovered that a positive goal would be to relax more and enjoy life as it is, not as it should be. She also found out that she was addicted to perfection and therefore felt like she never accomplished anything really worthwhile for herself.

Evaluate the goals or changes you have written down in terms of whether they are outer or inner goals. Usually the best results in life come from changing ourselves first. In this real sense, inner is prior to outer. You can rewrite your goals to include the negative blocks needing changing, the positive potentials needing actualizing, and the inner goals behind it all needing development.

Actualizing Our Goals

Now that we have become clearer on what we want, how do we really achieve these things?

* How realistic am I being about what I want?
* Yet, if I do not push for something which seems almost impossible will I ever reach my goal?

We actualize our goals by first becoming clear about them, often pushing back what we think to how we ultimately feel. One person felt her most central and most frustrating goal was to write. She planned, yet she did not write! When she explored in depth she found that her real core issue was that she felt she had never really fulfilled herself and done what she wanted. She had raised a family, but she experienced that as doing work for others.

Now she must do something for herself, she passionately stated, tears in her eyes. If she did not write she would feel like a failure.

What a struggle it was for her to see that the goal was not actually the writing, but the self-affirmation of meeting her own needs first, even at the expense of others.

In the long run it is more beneficial to meet one's own needs than to try to meet someone else's needs. The adult way is to become responsibly self-sufficient instead of muddling in other people's affairs as a substitute for dealing with your own stuff.

Commitment

Commitment is sustained choice in a given direction over a specific period of time. There is a certain knowledge and effectiveness which comes only through commitment to a project or purpose in life. Without commitment most of us would try to retreat when the going gets rough or when we start doubting. We need commitment as a structure within which to fight the regressive pull.

I will remain steadfast in my purpose no matter what tries to drag me backward.

What a beautiful intention to affirm in dealing with the regressive forces in life and in ourselves!

* To what am I ultimately committed in life?

* What is the more ultimate choice in every choice I make?

I may choose,

* To become realistic in all things.
* To achieve my own wholeness and unity of being.
* To live life to the full.
* To become devoted to an ultimate source other than ego.

What for you is an ultimate goal or direction in this life to which you can commit, and for how long can you stay committed? Will you really make the commitment? You do this on your own time and in your own way in your own silence. This is not a group ritual like baptism, or graduation. **You alone have the final choice about how you live your life and to what your life is centrally directed.**

We also need commitments, large and small, to give us experience to process. Sometimes it is simply necessary to commit to something, anything, to create greater involvement in life and to have new experiences to process. And we try not to give up the commitment when the going gets rough and the values seems impossible to realize. Nor do we let go of commitment when things are going well and we feel inflated by success and so also in danger of letting go of the real goal.

What is my goal and what will I do to achieve it?

Never forgetting that the opposites exist, that I may not achieve my goal as well as achieve it, at least I have committed myself to a process and this no one can take away from me even if my known goal is not successful.

What is my commitment and what am I willing and able to do to maintain it?

In Jesus' teaching there is a parable about a man who found a pearl of great price and sold everything he had to get it.

What am I willing to give up to have my goal? Write about this now. The greater the value the greater the price. **There are no bargains with God.** No person who is realistic would pay a price if what he or she is getting is worth less than what is being given up. We want new life, so of course we will sacrifice the old life, we will pay lesser for greater. No? We often have a hard time giving up the old? The ego does not like to leave the known and go into the unknown. It likes to rest on its laurels.

What is my goal and what more will I do to achieve it?

We will be more able to make the big changes in our lives if we practice little changes daily. There is the potential for newness and wholeness in every situation. So why hold on to the old any longer than you have to?

Create change in your life as well as continuity. Even now as you read this, experiment, make a change and deal with what happens.

The Best Way To Proceed With The Practices

The specific principles found in this book and in life become real for you through doing the practices on a daily basis.

I will change my life on a daily basis through choices and actions which have meaning for me.

You do not have to do the practices, of course. Each of us has choice in what we will do with our lives on a daily basis. We can drift with and react to the day. Or we can develop a strong and creative choice-making ego which structures and directs the life energy available to it. And how we determine each day will be how we live life. The results, the accomplishments, the life vitality and meaning, will come or not come through how you make your choices.

For many people the times after waking up in the morning and before going to bed are the most creative, open times and therefore good for retraining and developing your consciousness. Without doubt, how you begin and end your days makes a difference in the quality of how you live your day. Try it both ways and see for yourself the results.

Let yourself wake up grouchy and in a bad mood, dwell in it and call up all sorts of negative feelings and attitudes, such as "I don't give a damn," and then drift into your day reacting impulsively.

Or as a simple yet profound alternative, wake up and if you are in a foul or depressed mood, write about it in your journal or on a piece of paper, maybe recording a dream also. Then pick up this book and do one of the practices for yourself, and then take the most significant principle from the practice lesson and use it throughout the day. Will your day be significantly different? Evaluate before bedtime that night.

We can react to life or enact life, living its meaning to the core.

You may feel you are failing at the practices or not understanding parts of them. This is natural. Your only commitment is to continue despite any difficulties or regressive pulls.

I always have choice in every situation. I can use that choice to change my life.

Suggestions for Experiencing Maximum Benefit from Doing the Practices

1. Choosing any lesson which seems relevant, do one part of it each day if possible and keep doing lessons for as long as they evoke creative energy for you. Daily practice will mean that you are incorporating these principles and practices, as well as others which you come up with on your own, in your being and consciousness. However, you may wish to start by doing a lesson a week. Then choose how many days of the week and how many hours each week you will devote to it. Put your commitment on your calendar. You might also choose an unstructured approach. Keep this book by your bedside, in the bathroom, on the living room table and delve into it when drawn to it. Try not to put the book away on your bookshelf if you want to actively work with it.

2. Every day before falling asleep read over the lesson or practice you will do upon awaking the following morning. Read without doing anything unless you get evoked and need to process the energy. Then do that part of the lesson.

3. Upon awaking the next morning, record in a journal or on some paper any thoughts or feelings which come into your consciousness, including dreams. If you want to actively work with a special dream, use the techniques in the *Jungian-Senoi Dreamwork Manual.* Then read the practice lesson again and do one or two exercises which make sense to you, or do them all!

4. You determine how much time you devote to each lesson each day or week. Remember, you are changing your life. The amount of time you spend in this kind of psychological and spiritual activity will be returned to you many times over in increased effectiveness and direction in life. **We do not save time in life, we spend it wisely.**

5. Spend a few minutes in your relaxed state repeating to yourself the lesson's opening aphorisms and principles. Let them evoke thoughts and feelings of your own which you may choose to write down.

6. Each day ask yourself, DO I CHOOSE INTEGRATION? OR DO I CHOOSE TO RUN FROM CONFLICT?

7. Put the lessons's principles on cards and review them throughout the day. Apply them to everyone and everything. Allow play and humor to creep into your life, as well as courage and fortitude.

8. At the end of your day review, maybe in a free-flowing meditation, in a conversation with a friend or partner, or in a journal or word processing file, what has happened and not happened for you in working and playing with the lesson.

9. Go on to your next lesson. Simply read it before falling asleep, maybe asking for a dream on the subject.

10. Allow yourself not to do the lessons as well as to do them. Remember the opposites!

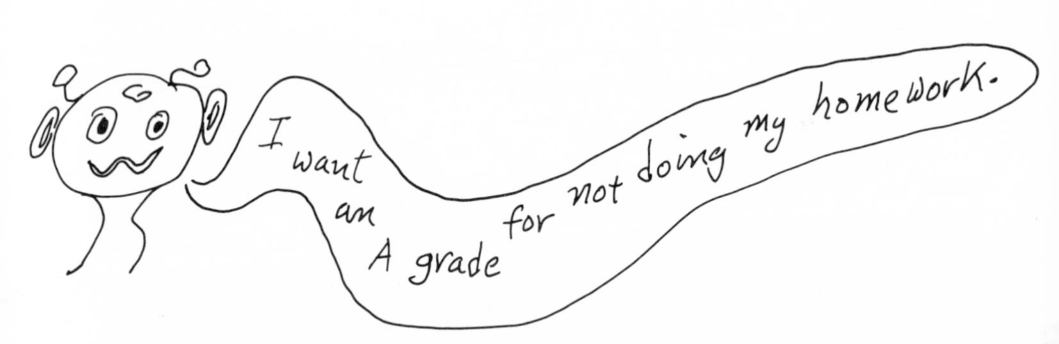

The Practices

In the same way I have developed habits for working and eating, in the same way I can develop psychological and spiritual practices for living a changed and more conscious life.

We will fool no one here. These are wonderful practices and principles for realizing oneself and achieving fulfillment, but they do require practice, which is repeated work at expression until you and I become skilled in using the approach.

You can learn much from a book. A book can change your life, especially if it is the product of already changed lives.

But the application of the approach is what is crucial to real transformation. Therefore we have included brief descriptions of the daily practices as well as the principles articulated in aphorisms, affirmations and intentions.

You will probably find yourself wanting to try things out. Do it. Do as much as you can on your own. And also join with friends.

You may want to set up for yourself and a friend a weekly meeting or meal together in which you share your experiences of the lessons you have both worked with on your own. This will be your "journey partner."

You may even want to form or be part of an ongoing group in which you do the lessons together and share and evaluate the results. This could be called a "personal transformation group."

We would like nothing better than that the principles and practices in this book become part of the relationship of many people, in friendships, families, and even work relationships. Successful relationships are based on renewal. Having a meaningful outside context to share can benefit both the individual and the relationship.

Life can only be lived at the Source

It's good for him.

your own sacred area for healing

SKW

Practice 1

LEAVING THE CASTLE—THE DEFENSE SYSTEM

"We defend ourselves against that which we are unwilling or unable to process."

Castles are beautiful, lovely to look at, perched high upon mountain tops. But they are also deadly, full of lonely towers for observing but not participating in the world, and full of dungeons down in the depths where the rejected sides of ourselves get imprisoned and tortured, creating pits of blood and shame beneath the throne.

And who reigns or tries to be supreme upon the throne? The ego of course, if it can, or even the inner parents if they have not been defeated and removed by the next generation.

Massive and glorious as it may seem the castle is a refuge from without and a prison for those within.

An Example

A few years ago I worked with a severely disturbed teenager who at age nine had been the youngest boy in a juvenile prison. For many years after we got him at our treatment center he showed no anger directly but was always stealing things. After much intensive work, at the onset of adolescent sexual development he began to get his anger out successfully. One time he physically fought me to a draw. Another time he went rampaging through the whole house where he lived with other disturbed teenagers breaking furniture and wielding threateningly a butcher knife. I was frightened but confronted him, secretly instructing another staff member I could trust to tackle him from behind. We took the knife away and, by holding him and taking him through a process for expressing anger and hurt, helped him get out that repressed rage he had stored up from a tragic childhood.

When he was 17 his rages became uncontrollable and he was sent to juvenile prison again to face reality. I, as his therapist, prescribed that he was not to have any cigarettes, to which he was addicted. He was being placed in absolute containment to experience his own emotions just as they were. I would visit him almost daily and we would have our talks on the nature of what he was going through.

After fourteen days in absolute confinement with only himself to deal with he realized that he did not have to break out any more. He had broken out of his defense system. He had made it. Walls did not scare him anymore. He could be with himself now. Even not being able to smoke did not matter.

He returned to us at the residential treatment center and a few weeks later he shared a dream.

I dreamed that the old witch who ruled the castle in which I was a prisoner had died and left me the keys to the castle. I now had a choice to become the ruler of the castle myself or take the keys, open the door, and leave it forever. I chose to leave the castle and found myself visiting a young couple in their small cottage where I fell asleep on the couch.

My heart is still moved by this dramatic transformation. He is now out in the world living as a successful and self-sustaining adult, and not in prison or in a mental hospital, where he would have ended up if he had not been subjected to therapeutic treatment based on working with the healing factors in the unconscious. Transformation can occur if we are committed enough to it as a process which leads to healing as the goal.

The Defense System

The castle has appeared in many other peoples' dreams that I have worked with over the years. Inevitably in therapy we find ourselves dealing with the defense system, that necessary mechanism we had to develop in childhood to keep from being overwhelmed and made crazy by our parents' and other adults' uses of power.

We defend ourselves from that which we are unwilling or unable to deal with and make conscious.

In childhood we developed ways to repress or put out of consciousness painful and terrifying feelings and experiences. We restricted ourselves. We killed ourselves a little or a lot. We withdrew into fantasy when things got too rough out there with our parents and the rest of the world. For each of us, the overwhelming trauma came, the alcoholic parent, the unexpected death or divorce, the sickness, the terror in the night, and we withdrew from feeling it fully.

When you cut off painful feelings you also cut off joyful feelings. It is a spiritual and psychological fallacy to think that you can train yourself to experience only good feelings. Remember the opposites.

What you repress in one area will assert itself in another.

In modern therapy, clients are often encouraged to experience and deal with painful feelings and experiences so that they can become free, not of pain, but of the necessity to repress pain and suffering. What was true in childhood need not be true in adult years. We can leave our fantasy system and our idealism, which we used to color our childhood reality, and accept the world and reality just as it is. We can deal with pain, and joy, and conflict, and enthusiasm, and passion, and all the great emotions and feelings if we will only commit ourselves to no longer repressing certain thoughts and feelings by escaping into fantasy or rationalism, but experiencing and processing whatever comes up.

An Example

Years ago in my early thirties I wanted to be a writer badly. It was the one thing in the world which mattered the most to me. My parents had been writers, my father a published poet and poetry anthologist who became well known. My parents had never thought I would be a writer but, no matter how I looked at it, I loved words and wanted to make my own mark in the literary world.

Yet I had many personal problems and a good deal of arrogance. My first marriage, which contained much potential, failed in part because I was too self-assured and did not seek therapeutic help when real difficulties developed between me and my wife.

After the divorce and my father's death I began to write in earnest a novel about young love. There were many intense feelings I wanted to express but somehow my ability with words was not enough to create magnificent and meaningful prose.

My next step was to go into therapy with an older woman who was also a writer. I thought I was starting therapy to overcome my writing blocks. But I quickly discovered that what I had seen as writing blocks was really my defense system strangling the life force trying to break through.

I also attended seminars given by this wise woman and her colleagues and out of that process decided to make a fundamental commitment to change my life. This I learned about in the workshops, but the actual commitment to follow the transformational source of my life I did alone, complete with the struggle to let go of the old and a simple ceremony of commitment which I devised for myself.

I had made a fundamental choice to follow integrative sources other than ego, but then I was soon to be tested. I can remember it just as clearly as the day it happened. I am sitting on a grassy hillside in San Francisco near where I lived at the time, working in my journal. I am facing the dilemma of whether I am using my unconscious to write or to grow and change personally. I know deep down in my heart that I will have to let go of the writing. It is the one thing that I would want to hold on to no matter what. I know also that a commitment to a healing source greater than ego means sacrificing exactly what I most want to keep. Or else the commitment has no meaning because I as ego will not have been able to let go of possessiveness and control.

I remember clearly writing—"All right, if I am never to write again so be it. What I want most is life. I will work directly with the core of my being and not use the unconscious or Self for anything other than what it wants from me."

I did not feel great joy at this sacrifice. It was not even a relief, though I realized its implications. I suffered the conscious loss but I knew I would hold to not following the compulsion to write again. For five years I did not write except in my journal or in a college paper.

The results of this commitment have been overwhelmingly beneficial, way beyond what I could have foreseen or hoped for. I began developing a flexibility and flow which allowed me to help transform real problems and live life abundantly. I was even able to let go of my therapist and training organization years later when the time was ripe. Nothing did I hold onto for long, as soon as I realized some new possessiveness, and so I was able to live many changes and produce new actualities in my life.

Why am I writing again? I never said I would never write. I gave up the compulsion to write. That if it was not meant for me to write I would not write. Writing was no longer the goal but merely a process. Five years later I was called upon by the treatment center where I worked to write a manual on meditation, therapy, and spiritual practice, which I did with trembling and hope that I could now find words to express what was significant and necessary to the project. The privately published book which I wrote was so moving to me that when I read it to the staff at the request of the director I cried at certain passages. I cried knowing that something needed and powerful was beginning to move through me. I was in awe and full of joy. What I had given up had come back to me transformed and potent in meaning.

And I must add, as far as my ego was concerned, it felt somewhat demeaned and non-literary that it had to write manuals and not great fiction. And I have been writing manuals ever since, as this book shows. Life came to me on its own terms.

The Practice

If you wish to make a commitment, even to a limited extent, the following commitment to leave the defense system is a major possibility. It is not done all at once. You do not step off into a new kind of saintliness. But you can decide to become clearer on the fundamental approach you want to take toward life. Such a commitment may be fourfold,

* To let go of the defense system as we learn about it,
* To allow and experience whatever comes up,
* To develop the skills and the support to process whatever comes up,
* And to commit oneself and one's ego to following a direction more whole, healing and wise than the ego itself alone can produce.

This is a commitment that one can make for life because, even in your inadequacy and confusion, what you want is life in all its fullness and meaning.

This is a commitment you can make in some form worked out by you which no one else need ever know. It is wise to keep counsel only with yourself and your own soul about certain core matters in life.

Whatever you do, no one will ever know directly about the commitment but you. It is a choice and a commitment which you alone make because you want a better life than you now have.

I alone have the fundamental choice about what I do with my life and what I ultimately serve.

If you want to pursue commitment further at some point, go over what is being said here and what it evokes for you. Then when you feel as ready as you can, make a choice and a commitment. This you may do in writing or also in some simple ceremony which you do alone in a place which has meaning for you. Focus on the following questions.

* To what are you committing?
* What are you giving up to make the commitment?
* For what period of time are you committing?

And finally, remember **I will remain steadfast in my purpose no matter what tries to drag me backward. Even myself.**

If such an action does not serve your purposes right now or you feel unready for any reason, then wait. You alone decide. Arrive at your own position on this fundamental life issue.

Working With Methods For Change

The commitment to let go of the defense system served as the beginning topic to this section because it is the natural basis upon which to carry through in doing these psychological and spiritual practices.

You do not, of course, have to make as fundamental a commitment as outlined here to do exercises. You can just move ahead with different ones and see what happens for you.

But will you really do the practices with your whole heart? Will you devote quality time to this most necessary of tasks, the working with your real self?

Practice 2

DEVELOPING FOCUS IN LIFE

"A single focus on what could go well instead of badly leads to greater accomplishment in reality."

What would it be like to be expressing yourself fully most of the time? Many of us have glimpsed this possibility of being so completely present to the moment that we know what is going on at deep levels and what to do about it. The trick is to learn how to develop this centered experience on a daily level and in the little things.

We practice single focus by seeking what is essential in each moment and living only that.

Example—Practicing Single Focus

I was having lunch in a cafe with a former client of mine who had made significant strides in getting established in the world and in his personal life. It was an informal place where you obtained your food at the counter and sat at little tables. During our animated conversation about our lives I seized the opportunity when I saw a space in the line of people to throw my empty paper plate closed up with leftover food in it through the line into the trash basket about six feet away. This was a conscious and sudden decision on my part which my lunch companion noticed. He commented immediately that I might have splattered leftover food on the floor or on people if I had missed.

"Yes, you are right," I replied. "But the point is that I did not miss. My focus, unlike yours, was totally on throwing my trash into the basket and not on what could go wrong. I think there is a principle here. If in life we focus on what could go wrong then we will not be focusing on what could go right and we will most likely go wrong and miss our opportunity."

He laughed and commented he had not realized that I was an athlete. It is true that I practice Aikido, a Japanese martial art, but I also practice wastepaper basket throwing. Unlike the purely physically oriented athlete, I am interested much more in my state of consciousness than in physical skill. I do not count how many times I hit the basket. I am aware only of how focused I am on the one goal, consciously excluding all that could go wrong and block that goal. I do not avoid thinking the negative. I consciously exclude it from the center of awareness with single focus.

My point with my friend was a reality one. I had thrown into the basket. That was the fact. How could he argue with that? If we adopt the principle of single focus we can actualize much more in life.

A single focus on what could go well instead of badly leads to greater accomplishment in reality.

The Method

We practice single focus by adopting life principles which work well in reality. Take one day this week and use one of these principles in everything you do. For example,

* I will say only what I really feel in a situation.
* I will work on first accepting, or opening up to, whatever happens to me before I interact with it.
* I will say No before saying Yes or No so that I may practice saying No in life.

Single focus, as used here, does not mean that I only concentrate on one thing at a time in my daily activities. Some of us are so scattered that we may need to narrow down our actions to only doing two or three things at once, but to do only one thing at a time, all the time, is the way of a boring plodder, completely predictable, who will come up with no surprises to delight, terrorize, or mystify.

In my personal example of wastepaper basket throwing I am practicing the life principle of acting with success in mind and not defeat, with single-pointedness and not "divided mind."

At the back of this book is a list of life principles. You might take one of these and practice it throughout your day to give yourself single focus, focus which starts from your inner core and permeates all that you do.

Practice 3

DISCOVERING ATTITUDES

"An attitude is an unconscious context for choice."

The primary reason to begin making our attitudes conscious is to free ourselves from being unconsciously governed by them. We want to open up the arena of what we can do and express in life. We do not want to be confined to narrow definitions of reality or behavior given by someone else, perhaps hundreds of years ago. An amazing fact is that most people seem to live by attitudes passed down to them generation by generation, as if those personal laws lived in the past are necessarily true for us today.

What Is an Attitude?

An attitude is an unconscious context for choice. An attitude is a personal rule for how to live life. "The world is a good place to live in" is an attitude given to us from somewhere. Others may have the opposite attitude. What is common to those with both attitudes is that they believe them as the truth and act accordingly.

We use the term, "attitude," where some people might also use "belief," as in "I believe that when you do good to others they will do good to you." We also might speak of a "belief system." So sometimes "belief" will describe the same dynamic as "attitude." We use only the word, "attitude," in this book to keep things simple.

Why Are Attitudes Unconscious?

It's easier to make choices automatically rather than get into a big ethical discussion with oneself every time we want to make a choice. Also it is easier to just grab something as the truth than to see its opposite as also relevant to life. Identification with one attitude or opposite causes unconsciousness. The main reason attitudes are automatic and unconscious is that they were largely taught to us by our parents and society long before we had the reasoning power to think for ourselves. Parents, naturally enough, want to make us into images of themselves, and so they give us their own rules about what life is and how it should be lived. They assume that what is true for them will be true for us. This itself is an attitude rather than an absolute.

The trouble with living attitudes unconsciously is that the ones we have received may be contradictory and no longer appropriate to a changing reality. At one point it was somehow wrong to have sex before marriage or to live with someone without getting married. That has begun to change. A different attitude is emerging which says that people can handle their sexuality without having to be married to contain it. Perhaps we have more consciousness and choice-making power today than ever before.

Where Do Attitudes Come From?

Most people think that attitudes come from God. God for them is some absolute truth and power somewhere ruling the universe and handing out laws to live by to leaders on mountain tops.

An Example

"It's wrong to hurt other people."

"Who told you that?"

"It's wrong. It just is."

"I know you feel that way, but who said it? Who gave you this truth? Did it come direct from God? Or from your parents? Or where?"

"Well, I don't know. Isn't it always wrong to hurt people? You wouldn't deliberately hurt someone, would you?"

"Yes, I have done it many times and I suspect I will do it again."

"You're not a good person."

"I scare you, you mean. Now you are afraid of me because I don't have the same attitude you do. Let's look at reality. When might it be beneficial to deliberately hurt someone?"

And so goes the dialogue. Most people assume certain absolute truths. We are calling those assumptions attitudes. Attitudes often come from experiences in childhood. Abused children who have been physically hurt over and over again grow up afraid of being hurt by others. For them it would be difficult to see that hurting someone can sometimes be positive. **Our traumas produce defense systems whose defenders are the attitudes we possess**. So changing attitudes often means dealing with the traumas of the past and the defensiveness towards life they produced.

What Can We Do About Our Attitudes?

Some attitudes are difficult to make conscious, let alone change. An attitude itself may be a defense system created to help keep us safe from certain experiences in life. If we have been traumatized by anger in us or directed towards us we may have an attitude that anger is bad or should not be openly expressed. But anger is not good or bad. Anger is anger. Anger is a reality when it's there and when it comes up. Yes, I am proposing another more realistic attitude here, one which suggests that anger expression can have a positive place in the range of human emotions.

The process is to make unconscious attitudes conscious, evaluate their effectiveness and consistency with how life really is, and then accept or change them according to your values in life.

We work at realizing the attitudes and patterns behind our choices to bring choice to our choices. It takes time and courage to risk new ways of approaching life. But the changes can be effective and produce new experiences of meaning and fulfillment. We also seek out those life principles which make sense to us and commit ourselves to living by them instead of by unconscious attitudes. **Values are attitudes consciously realized**. A value is itself a context for choice, a way of affirming a certain principle about how life works. You can have unconscious attitudes but not unconscious values. In order to have values you must consciously choose them and choose to live by them. And may your values be consistent with reality and not be pie-in-the-sky idealism or seeds of unconscious religious or political fervor.

If we adopt the life principle that "It is better to sacrifice the old so that the new may be born," then this will clash with an unconscious attitude that "It is safer to stay with the known than to go into the unknown." But is it safer? Sometimes Yes, but many times No. The issue is to bring choice to the attitude so that we may choose either way in order to deal with life as it is, not as we would want it to be. If I value safety above risk in life I will not be able to adopt the new principle articulated above. So working with attitudes and principles does bring us forthrightly to the shores of what we value in life. We can choose to modify or adopt new values, or we can choose to stay the way we are and see what life does to us in this state of inflexibility.

You don't have to choose change in your life, but will life change you anyway, willy-nilly, whether you want to or not?

The Practice—Discovering Your Attitudes

1. Focus on a current issue in your life. Develop questions about it and the various choices you could make. List also the feelings which come up for you regarding each of your choices.

* Example—I want to find a new place to live.

What's wrong with your present place? What comes up for you when you focus on moving? What kind of place would you like to have? Is your vision of what you want consistent with your means and reality? What are your choices? Which choice is the scariest for you?

2. Take the strongest feeling and work with it to discover the attitudes which might be producing the feeling.

* Example—I'm really most scared about moving to a new area.

What images do you see when you experience that feeling? What questions does it raise for you? How would you state your feeling in a positive or negative sentence?

How about, "I won't find new friends if I move to a different area."? What assumption are you making about yourself here?

"That I'm not able to make new friends."

Is this actually true for you?

"No, I actually make friends with certain people quite easily."

Then why are you afraid?

"It's new. That's all!"

Is that your basic fear?

"Yes, that's it."

Is it all right to be scared of new things?

"I do seem to have an attitude, don't I, that I shouldn't be scared of changes? Maybe it's all right to be frightened? I know I'll go ahead anyway if it feels right to me."

The possible old attitudes were, "I don't make friends easily." "I won't find new friends if I move." "It's not all right to be frightened of changes."

The new, more conscious attitudes to live by are, "I can find friends wherever I go." "I am a likable person." "It's all right to be afraid of changes in my life." "I can move ahead even when I'm afraid." "I don't have to be afraid of new things."

A basic life principle underlying the new attitudes could be, "The future always holds new possibilities for growth and life." Or, "I must let go of the past in order to actualize the future."

3. As we have seen from what developed in the above example, you can discover and create new attitudes based on your own inner wisdom and life principles which you value.

4. Another way of discovering unconscious attitudes is to first describe your behavior or reactions to a situation, then generalize statements about it.

* Example—I receive a parking ticket and become angry.
* Process—I describe my feelings until I get down to the most basic essence of the thing.

"I'm upset because I'm worried about my money situation and this is just one more blow to my finances. I was stupid not to put more money in the meter. Maybe I can't handle everything I'm doing right now. I'm not perfect but I have to be better than I am to get everything done right in my life. I hate the system for taking my money."

And to generalize—"I'm afraid of life right now. I'm afraid I really might not make it, that things will go against me. I must have an attitude that life is barely surviving, life is a jungle. I need a new attitude that I always have everything I need to handle any situation to the best of my ability."

5. Don't try to discover all your major attitudes at once, of course. But this practice is one that you can do anywhere every day of the year. You can listen to yourself as you talk. You can point out to your friends, "That's an attitude, not a God-given statement of absolute truth." Ask yourself continually, "Now, where did that come from?" Sorting out one's attitudes I find is much more fun than playing Scrabble or other information games like Trivia. Each to his or her own. I prefer to play the game of life.

I'm Judge Attitude
I'm in Charge!
I want the Freedom to choose ...
SKW

THE TWENTY-FIVE MOST DESTRUCTIVE ATTITUDES PLAGUING PEOPLE EVERYWHERE

Caution! Do not study these attitudes unless you are willing to transform at least some of them in yourself. These and other reality-denying attitudes are the bars to many an imprisonment by fate. Drink deeply and purge yourself of your unreality.

1. The future is likely to turn out worse than the present.
2. The way to be successful is to focus only on the positive in life.
3. Working on my own survival is the only realistic goal in life.
4. Focusing on love and light prevents evil and darkness from taking over in my life.
5. The way to win struggles is to be better than your adversaries.
6. There is one truth, one right way, in life and I can know it.
7. If people do not like me I will fail in what I am doing.
8. I must have outside authorities to tell me what is best for my life.
9. I am not really capable of dealing creatively with any situation in life.
10. The real world is what happens out there rather than also inside myself.
11. It is always wrong or dangerous to cause others pain.
12. It is better that I should suffer than that others should suffer.
13. What is real is only what I can concretely perceive with my senses.
14. It is right to prefer pleasure and avoid pain.
15. It is better in all things to be good rather than bad.
16. The way to let go and relax is to make oneself unconscious.
17. If we keep some feeling or perception out of consciousness we will not have to deal with it.

18. My conscious ego is the center of my life and what I should choose for in making choices.
19. Focusing on things outside onself, such as work and children, is necessarily healthy and positive.
20. There is only one God or focus for all of life and everything else is to be excluded as unreal or bad.
21. God is all powerful and only good.
22. My choices do not really matter to the universe or anyone else besides myself.
23. All is relative. There is really no meaningful way in anything. It is only what each person chooses as right that matters.
24. We can build a reasonably secure future by what we do in the present.
25. There is life after death and therefore it does not really matter what we do with our lives. We don't have to live life as if this is the only life we have.

Powerful? This can be quite a dose of medicine. You may disagree that some of these attitudes are unrealistic or unreal. Perhaps then you can rewrite an attitude as a positive life principle for yourself? **History is ultimately the record of the clash of life principles among peoples.** Each one of us plays a part in the universal struggle. Your consciousness and mine are the specific arenas for humankind's ongoing struggle to make itself more aware and active in how life and its supreme potentials really work.

Each one of us is a commandeered warrior in the battleground of life. You can choose to go unconscious and only focus on immediate needs and desires, and let that magnificent brain and heart go to waste, or you can choose to enter the struggle, make conscious the life-defeating attitudes sleepily handed you, and transform them or substitute for them new life principles and values to live by.

As a way of working with these attitudes say them, notice what they evoke in you, play with them, discuss them with friends, work them out of your system so that new principles can be substituted for them as a way to transform life.

IT CAN HAPPEN AGAIN, SO BE READY.

Practice 4

CHANGING ATTITUDES THROUGH AFFIRMATIONS

"I am always changing to meet a new reality."

As we have already described elsewhere, our life actions and choices are mostly based on unconscious attitudes or contexts out of which we make our choices. These attitudes were often taught to us over and over again by our parents and society, both of whom wanted us for some reason to have the same attitudes they had.

But each person and each generation must reserve for itself the right to reevaluate and discard or change the attitudes given it by the parents and previous generation. For besides attitudes, the parents and society give the next generation the problems which they themselves could not or did not solve. New solutions require new attitudes or new ways of seeing reality. The gift which each next generation brings into the world is their openness to change, since they are not already loaded down with outworn and inappropriate attitudes and values.

Would that the older generations would let go a lot more and give the younger generations more power and more say in changing things. A culture's health can be measured by its willingness and ability to let go of yesterday's ways and values in the face of tomorrow's problems and potentials.

We also want to reevaluate present ingrained attitudes to see if they are consistent with reality as well as with our highest values. Reality is always changing and our best protection is to change with it. Why resist the new by hanging onto the old? Yet everybody does this and wastes a hell of a lot of time and effort in doing so. Maturity is less a gift than the result of flexible and flowing work.

I am always changing to meet a new reality.

Procedure for Creating Affirmations

1. First unearth some fundamental attitude in yourself, such as "the future is likely to be worse than the present" and evaluate it regarding its realism and meaning for your life. To get at attitudes look at your choices and actions and discover what statements, laws, values or principles are serving as the context for your choices here.

2. Next rewrite your present attitude in a more realistic and positive light. "The future is likely to be worse than the present" becomes "the future is likely to be as positive as the present and sometimes more positive." How do you feel about this rewrite? How do you contrast the original statement and the new one?

3. Write or say over and over to yourself the new more realistic and meaningful attitude and see what results. You might write the new attitude in a left hand column and write anything evoked, no matter what, in a right hand column. This is what Leonard Orr calls "the negative mass." It is the repository of all your former training and must be evoked out of you in order for you to change and really use the new attitude effectively. Statements might spontaneously come out like the following. "No, the future will be awful, at least for me anyway. I have always had bad luck."

See how persuasive former conditioning is? Now write a new statement which somehow combines your affirmation and the negative mass it evoked, such as follows,

"I am more and more able to see that the future may be as good as or better than the present."

We keep re-saying the new affirmation, or writing it, until we have cleared out the negative mass. We have then retrained ourselves, and what an accomplishment that is! Repeating affirmations counterbalances the many, many times an original attitude was said over and over to us. We are retraining our consciousness.

4. Another creative practice is to go around continually changing unrealistic and meaningless affirmations as you perceive them in yourself and in others.

A Conversation About an Attitude

"I'm tired."

"That's an attitude."

"What do you mean attitude. I feel exhausted."

"This is what you are telling yourself. No wonder you are tired. What if you told yourself, 'I'm in the process of renewing myself,' when you felt low energy?"

"No, I prefer to say I'm tired when I am tired."

"Suit yourself. I was going to ask you to go dancing with me..."

"Oh, in that case, I would love to go dancing with you! Let's go. I feel energized again."

"I like your spirit! I feel better myself."

Do we dare say that most of the time we think we are tired we are simply blocked in our energy flow and need to find a new place within ourselves from which to act?

The secret of renewal is not collapse but change to a different way or area of self-expression.

5. Here are some life denying or reality denying attitudes afflicting the world's people today. Which ones inhabit your psyche? How would you say them in your own words? How would you rewrite them as affirmations?

* Things will go wrong if I risk developing something new.
* It's wrong to hurt other people, even to do something positive for myself.
* I can't change.
* I can't handle it.
* Being happy is what life is all about.
* The future is likely to be worse than the present.
* Most people will do you in if given a chance.
* Life is so difficult that I can barely survive.

Make it an ongoing life pursuit to keep identifying attitudes that are still ingrained in you. Then transform, transform!

Practice 5

CHANGING ATTITUDES BY ADOPTING NEW LIFE PRINCIPLES

"Values are attitudes consciously realized."

Life principles are statements reflecting how life really works, for example, **the more you hide from something the more it will attack you.**

This can also be seen as an attitude or context out of which we make certain choices. Values are attitudes consciously realized. In other words, our values and life principles must be consciously articulated to be put into action through intentions. Attitudes themselves are mostly unconscious and probably the more unconscious they are the more unrealistic they are. We tend to repress what does not work, or what works all too well but against us.

We formulate and adopt life principles because we want to live effectively and meaningfully in this reality. We are not interested in mere survival or flight from pain. Fantasyland is for all those who choose to remain unconscious. We want reality and much of it. We want to live in the real world. We want to grow up and mature, making choices in a world inhabited by the opposites.

Procedure

1. Reflect for yourself and write a list of what are the most important current life principles by which you are living.

How do you evaluate these?

2. Choose for yourself the life principles by which you would like to live. You might have to focus in by dividing up the listing into subject areas of your life like Relationship, Productivity, Spirituality, etc. Which life principle seems central to them all? Make a hierarchy diagram of your life principles. You might pick ones from this book or elsewhere.

3. Choose a life principle you would like to work on in your life right now and restate it as an affirmation or two and as several intentions for action. Try these out in reality over the next week and see what results.

For example, if you have an unconscious attitude that "it is better to say Yes than No," then you will not be able to say No when you need to protect yourself. A new, more realistic life principle to adopt would be "we need to say No as well as Yes in life as the occasion demands." This is your new affirmation to use in breaking down and transforming your old attitude. An intention, or commitment to action, would be "I will practice saying No first to every request, even if I say Yes after. This will strengthen my ability to say No and increase my ability to choose."

Practice 6

ACTUALIZING INTENTIONS

"I will act to achieve my values
this and every
week of my life,
as the potentials become
known to me."

Changing Attitudes Through Intentions

We can change our behavior by transforming old and outworn attitudes into new ones. We change the contexts out of which we make our choices. But it is often not enough to simply create affirmations and change attitudes. We must act.

What does it profit anyone to know the creative thing and not do it? I shall know you by your actions and not your beautiful words. I shall know myself not by what I think but by what I act on. I will need courage to risk, skills to be effective, and a potential ripe for actualization in tune with my choices.

I am more and more willing to test myself by putting what I believe into action. This is my affirmation.

I will act to achieve my values this and every week of my life as the potentials become known to me. This is my intention.

The test of a value is the result produced when it is put into action through intention. Our intentions test our ability to perceive and be effective in reality. Not what I simply intend to do but what I carry out in life.

I will make my intentions specific and capable of being acted upon and realized within a definite amount of time.

Example

A few years ago I worked with a beautiful woman who came to me because she had had several flying dreams and wanted to know what they meant. It turned out that her flying dreams often took her into religious situations in which she would receive things from shaman women, children, etc. But what did she herself do with what she received?

After a couple of sessions she began revealing that she was in a sexual relationship with a man who was extremely jealous of her, a boxer with a repressed anger problem that made her fearful.

She wanted to leave him but could not, was the way she put her problem. We spent many sessions going over what she could do with her life. Was it right to leave him? Could she even leave him? What if he found her and killed her? He had guns. She kept it secret that she was coming to a therapist. Maybe she really loved him and needed to change herself. I as counselor and therapist could not tell her what choices to make. I was not living her life. But one day I said to her in a state of real inspiration and feeling, "When are you finally going to come down off your cross and take action?" I was tired of her wishes and wanted her to take action however she saw fit.

That was our last session together. When she missed our next appointment I called and got the recorded message, "service discontinued with no new number."

I assumed that she had moved to another state as she had talked of doing, that she had taken action at last.

It is by carrying out our intentions that we change life.

Procedure

1. Look at some recent event, pattern of events, or situation in your life that troubles you. *For example, I don't have enough money.*

2. Describe the situation fully, either writing it or telling it to yourself.

3. What feelings emerge about yourself, the others involved, and life in general? *I feel helpless. I feel envious of everybody else. I feel resentful toward life. I feel mistreated.*

4. Formulate a sentence, or several, expressing your attitudes. *I can't take good care of myself and shouldn't have to. Everybody else is better equipped than I am. Life is unfair to me.*

5. Watch for these attitudes in your life. Learn to recognize them as they crop up in your daily activities. Begin to divest them of their power by catching them and identifying them as "only attitudes."

6. Restate them in affirmation style. *I am learning to take better and better care of myself. I can use those other people as models. Life is full of opportunities.*

7. Then repeat an affirmation to yourself several times, letting come to you at the same time ways you can live and test the new attitude or value. For example, if your affirmation is "I am more and more able to deal with fear in my life," repeat this several times and sometimes suggestions for actions will follow, such as calling people back up after a conversation and telling them the things you haven't said out of fear.

8. Formulate a specific intention, and carry it out. Set periods of time for taking action.

9. Evaluate. Does your affirmation still reflect your intention and the results which came? If not, modify your affirmation or intention. What new attitudes or life principles come out of the results of your intentions?

Practice 7

THE ART OF CREATIVE CHOICE-MAKING

"What we choose is what we become."

The Contexts which Underlie Our Choice-Making

There is no such thing as a pure choice without its context. We choose, we direct energy one direction and not another, but we also have a context, or preference, out of which we make that choice. Every choice has its context. For some reason, or because of some feeling, we choose to go one way and not another.

Attitudes are the unconscious contexts for choosing. If I have an attitude, either known or unknown to me, that I am a poor chooser in life, then I will more than likely be making poor choices because this is the context I operate from. Change your context and you change your choice. This is why we have spent time on attitudes, affirmations, and intentions. We need to make conscious our unconscious contexts for choice and then rework and change these contexts so that we may live more effective and fulfilling lives.

What is the ultimate basis for you in making your choices? Each of us has a core context, a final authority out of which we make choices. One person says it feels right for her, and may spend years in feeling-expression types of therapy. Another adopts certain values or life principles, such as choosing for wholeness in every situation.

What we choose is what we become. But also we choose out of what we have already become. The trick is to break the barriers of the past. We break open our unconscious contexts for choice so that we may choose more fully in life.

Who knows if it is better to choose on the basis of feeling or intellect, or some combination of both? It might be that feelings come out of attitudes. I will react positively to something if I have an attitude that it is positive. So the approach used here is first to make conscious our unconscious contexts for choice and then to choose those we want to have as a basis for choice-making. We choose what we become.

Your chosen contexts for choice need to be consistent with reality. All the positive thinking in the world may not save you if negative things exist in life. If you have adopted an attitude of "think only love," "think only positive," then you will be ill equipped to deal with the destructive in life on its own terms.

The choices you make based on a particular attitude will serve as reality tests for it. What was the result of your choice? Did it confirm or negate the attitude in question? How will you adjust your ideas in the face of this new information?

The Practice For Making Creative Choices

1. Identify a life issue around which you need to make a choice. What has you excited? What are all the questions about it? What is the issue behind the issues? Keep pressing yourself back. Now what is behind that, and that, and that?

2. After formulating your issue in questions, develop it also as a number of possible choices. What is the most fundamental choice behind all the other choices? What is the inner choice involved which affects you directly? What is the outer aspect of the choice which affects the situation and others?

3. After working with the choices, next list the possible consequences. Make a list of both negative and positive consequences which might result. How do they weigh up? Do they balance each other out? Is there more weight in one list than in the other? Are you committed and able to deal with the negative, and positive, consequences which might result? Evaluate how committed you are to handling all eventualities.

4. What is the edge of risk for you? We may know a certain choice is right but be unwilling to make it because of our own resistance. We may be afraid. We may not want to change. We may doubt ourselves. You are making a choice to risk, to sacrifice the known for the unknown. What will you have to sacrifice in order to carry out your choice? An identification? A self-image? How do your resistances to this sacrifice appear? List the sacrifices and the resistances.

5. We may just want to rest, take it easy, and let someone else or fate make our choices for us. This is called the regressive pull. Describe it in words as it comes up around your choice. List also all the No's you will need to say in order to say Yes to your one choice.

6. Clarify positive and negative motivation. Negative motivation is the urge to avoid unpleasant consequences. What if you did not make what you know is the right choice in this situation? What would happen to you? It is perfectly valid to give yourself a kick in the ass to get moving. If you don't make your choice now it will be made for you one way or another. How much better to consciously take hold of your own destiny. So goes the reasoning about negative motivation. Positive motivation is allowing oneself to be inspired by the process of actualizing a new potential. Both positive and negative motivation can help us overcome the regressive pull so that we may strongly choose in life.

7. Find the more ultimate context for choice. Every choice is an immediate choice and an ultimate choice. We create ourselves by our choices. How I make choices determines how I live my life. At some point you may want to consciously commit yourself to a more ultimate choice you can continually make and re-make in all the specific choices of your life. An over-arching choice developed in this book is the intention to enhance wholeness in every specific choice I make. Each of us decides, consciously or unconsciously, what is that more ultimate choice to which we devote our lives. Better to know it and live it than to drift on muddy waters for the rest of our existence here.

8. After clarifying your own position, consider other points of view in the situation. Others may be involved. How might your decision affect them? You may also be using resources such as a therapist or teacher, dreams, intuitions, the tarot or the I CHING, meditation, artwork, journalwork, and prayer to expand your perspective. It is best to get as clear as you can before consulting outside sources. You may then change your position in order to include a larger whole, but you are starting with a sense of yourself, rather than trying to get an "authority" to make your choice for you.

9. When the time is ripe, choose, and discover the outcome. There is a time for choice, a point of maximum ripeness. To choose to actualize the new potential before the tension has developed enough often aborts the process or gives birth to a lesser thing. To over-wait out of fear and paralysis, or the unwillingness to sacrifice resistance, may give you little or nothing. A potential in life will have passed you by. We all know this feeling about the opportunities we have missed in life. Some we were not ready for. Others we had the choice to actualize or not actualize. Therein lies the agony and nostalgia for the past. We will know when the potential is ripe by our feeling for it and our intuition. You will just know. We need to be open to guidance for a thing to happen at this level.

10. Deal with the outcome. If positive results come in, do we accept them whole-heartedly? With results comes responsibility! And if the consequences are painful, remember it is all right to fail. We had to risk the negative to go for the positive. Every negative result is an opportunity to learn. We can always make new choices, even reverse a direction if we deal fully with the consequences of our present choice-making.

11. Evaluate your choice and its consequences. What further have you learned about the process? What does the experiece say about you? What would you have done differently? Does anything block your accepting fully the way things happened? What is the meaning of what resulted for you? Through finding the meaning we redeem the situation. What is your next choice, and how will you make it?

Example—Applying the Choice-Making Process to Abortion

She is a seventeen year old woman who after the pregnancy test finds that she is about eight weeks pregnant. She loves children but does not want to have a child this early in her life. She sees her choices as either having an abortion soon or having the child and giving it up for adoption, thereby earning $10,000 and all expenses paid. She does not see herself keeping the child, but is worried that if she had the child she would not be able to let it go for adoption.

Following our "Practice for Making Creative Choices," she lists the questions about her problem. She is working with a counselor trained to be neutral in order to help her consider the many sides of an issue and come to her own decisions.

Why does she even have an issue? What is she upset about? What is she not clear about? Does she have good practical information on the alternatives? What are her values? What support and opposition does she have from those close to her?

Where she is upset is where she is unclear or ambivalent. What is the issue behind the issues? Is it that she does not like to kill life, period? Is she most afraid of never having children again if she gives this one up, either through abortion or through adoption?

At the beginning of her choice-making process she cannot think straight and quickly realizes that she has a lot of anger around being pregnant. It comes as a shock to her. She is angry with the man for saying it would be all right, he'd pull out in time. She is angry with herself for believing him and going along with it in the heat of sexual excitement. She is angry with her parents for not giving her more structure.

She expresses the anger, really venting herself, so that she can release it and get to the reality at hand. She is pregnant and must do something about it.

Her issue now becomes whether to have the child and give it up for adoption, or have an abortion in the next week. Her one certainty is that she does not want to be a mother this early in her life. It would not be fair to herself or to the child. She has too much to do these next few years. She wants to travel. She sees that she must be educated to have a good job. She does not want to enter motherhood and marriage without a career of her own to keep her from being dependent at any time in her life.

She lists the outcomes of bringing her pregnancy to term and giving the baby up for adoption.

On the positive side, she would be bringing new life into the world, making another couple extremely happy, having a birth experience, earning money for travel or college, and pleasing her anti-abortion parents.

On the negative side, the man who made her pregnant would have an excuse to hang around her because she was carrying his child. She does not want to relate to him any more. She would find it difficult to give up a child of her own flesh, once it was born. She would always wonder about the child, where it was, how it was doing. She would have to have that kind of suffering for years. And what if something was wrong with the child or she died in delivery? A rare chance, but still . . . . And she would have to take a good nine months out of her regular life, and then get her body back in shape again. Men like tight vaginas, so she heard, and hers would be more open after the birth.

If she had an abortion soon she could go on with her life pretty much as she was now living it. There would be a minimum of hassle. She had not planned to get pregnant and would be very careful from now on. She had learned her lesson.

On the negative side, having an abortion would upset her parents if she told them about it. She would not have to tell them, since she could go to the women's clinic with complete confidentiality. She would feel bad and would always wonder what her child would have been like. But then again she could have a child when she had the right man as a father and lover, and she herself had a career. Yes, she was stopping a life, but she had a right to her own body, she felt, and that was it. The money for giving the child up for adoption would be nice but not essential to her pursuing her career. She would work part time when she went to college, and receive help from her parents.

The edge of risk for her would be that any way she chose, the results were both positive and negative. She had a tendency to avoid pain. That is why she was not sure she could actually let go of the child once it was born.

She might decide that getting an abortion was the simplest choice she was capable of making at this time in her life.

Yet, she could have the child and either keep it or give it up for adoption.

She consulted the Source Readings using synchronicity. The reading she obtained said,

> *From the beginning you have known that you have a single purpose to achieve in life.*
> *Why be so loaded down in the morass and minor issues of experience?*
> *Focus your energy.*
> *Make the most central choices and you will succeed in what you are meant to do.*

This reading astounded her and made her feel that it was right to get an abortion now so that her energy could be focused on a single purpose in life. This experience was teaching her to take care of herself more. It was almost as if she had unconsciously tried to give her life a focus by getting pregnant. From now on she would have to be more focused on what her next steps in life should be.

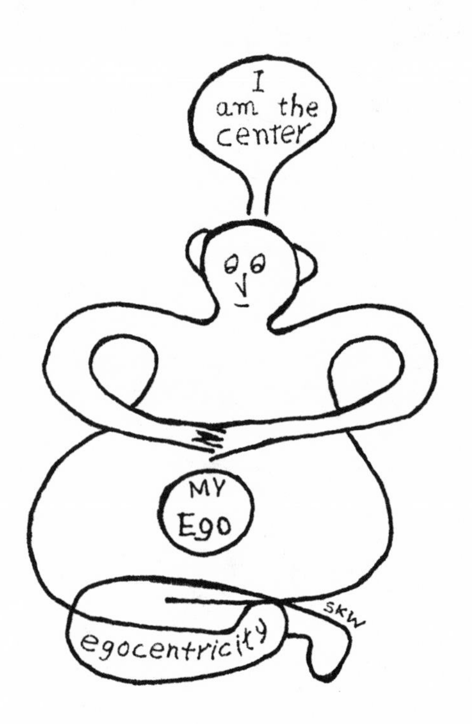
I am the center
MY Ego
egocentricity
SKW

Practice 8

DEALING WITH EGOCENTRICITY

"The price for egocentricity is death, not life."

How do you resonate or react to the following statements:

"Thank you for opposing me. That was just what I needed to get me off my high horse."

"You know, I think your criticism of me is right. I am like that, and I'm working on it.

"Thank you for causing me pain. I was getting too complacent."

"You really upset me, I hate you and I thank you for it."

"Thank God I did not get my way. I can relax now."

As a simple direct exercise, which of the above statements do you most react against and why? What does this say about yourself?
Would you like to have the following typical statements to deal with? Do you habitually come up with these yourself?

"No I didn't."

"You did that!"

"It's not my fault."

"I don't think I did it."

"I did not!"

"I had to because..."

"Go to Hell, anyway!"

"I did the best I could."

"I will not let you make me into a bad person."

What are your reactions here? Which do you identify with and use? Why? What characterizes all these statements?

Obviously, the ego does identify with and defend itself and its point of view. This is the basis for egocentricity, the focusing on oneself to the exclusion of anyone else or any other points of view.

Work to recognize, get familiar with, and then give up your egocentricity, so you can let more of life in, so you can give up the need to control everything, and gain the ability to relate to all things, so that you can follow and actualize sources more vital and meaningful than the ego alone can possess.

Example

I once attended a birthday dinner with a group of people who lived communally in the same house. I shall never forget one woman, a new member, who immediately when dinner was ready began helping herself. She took what she wanted of the delicacies regardless of others and was already eating her food before some had even served themselves. Plenty of food was on the table, so none of us were in danger of going hungry by her actions. It was just that she had no time to be gracious or interested in others. Her sense of timing about life seemed off. Her principle obviously was that you had to push for what you could get out of life and to deny yourself anything was false modesty.

She made a successful career out of similar actions. She accomplished the goals she had set for herself. Years later I met the woman again and still she was overly pushy. But this time I could tell that the confidence born of inflation had gone out of her eyes. She was a lonely woman, old before her time and from what I could tell had no intimate friendships.

Her egocentricity was killing her humanity. I immediately sensed her problem and could not help subtly communicating my awareness. I was open to our being real with each other, but she avoided me. I had found her egocentricity and the vulnerability behind it. The lesson is clear. **The price of egocentricity is death, not life.** Who wants to lose their essential humanity?

Procedure

1. Write out some conversational statements of yourself acting non-egocentrically. Practice saying and acting on these statements in daily life and see what results.

2. Write out also some typical egocentric statements you or your acquaintances use. These may be statements based on roles you identify with, or simply things you tell yourself and others to make you feel good about yourself. Then rewrite these statements into non-egocentric ones such as, "Thank you for upsetting me. This is just what I needed to let go of some stuff." Practice them, one at a time, in daily life.

3. Refer to the section in this book on the three types of egocentricity, 1) that of superiority, 2) that of inadequacy, 3) that of self-will. How would you describe yourself in relation to all three? Which egocentricities in other people make you angry or cause you to deny things about yourself?

Have a friend accuse you of each egocentricity and study how you react. Then create positions and statements which change the egocentricity into more of a wholeness pattern. For example, "Yes, I do think a lot of myself, but I also feel inadequate and just plain confused at times. But I do like feeling good about myself."

A Conversation

"Yes, of course I tend to dominate, and I'm working on it. Just tell me to shut up if I go on too much."

"But what if you get angry?"

"I probably will get angry for a second or two. But I might laugh also. Try me out. What's wrong with anger? That's just my ego hurting and purifying itself. I can take it, can you?"

"I don't know. You've been such a bully. I may try it out, depending on how I feel. It's really your responsibility."

"Yes, I know. But I'm asking for help and I feel I do have an effect on you."

"All right, I hear you. Let's drop this conversation and get on to our next thing."

"Okay. I can play ball."

Practice 9

DISIDENTIFYING FROM ARCHETYPES

"To play many roles in life
without identifying with any
contributes to wholeness."

This will not be easy. The ego needs its self-identity, or feels it does. Most often the ego will disidentify from archetypes only when forced to. A child leaves home early. A wife leaves her husband. The boss fires us. The business goes broke. Many of these calamities only happen because we insist on remaining identified with archetypes. And because we remain identified, we remain unconscious.

Identification is embodying one opposite to the detriment of the other. I identify with being a mother and cannot assume the father role at times or cannot even relate to my husband as lover-companion, a distinctly different role from the nurturing, giving mother role.

We disidentify to relate through choice and consciousness to the archetype and its opposite. Or fate intervenes and knocks us out of our identifications. A martial artist identifies with a heroic image only to have his arm broken accidentally in a bout with another martial artist. Another teaches masculinity and a strong father image only to have his son die by drowning. Or on an everyday level, the very day we are feeling really competent about our life is the day we lose our keys and cannot get into the house. If we go archetypal with our identifications, the archetype will take its toll.

I am not an archetype. I relate through choice to archetypes.

In terms of wholeness, then, I want to free myself up from my identifications as well as my compulsions in order to make choices which honor and integrate all sides of myself.

I am an arena for the archetypes needing differentiation and integration within my life.

The ego identifies with its *persona* and rejects and represses the *shadow*. We build persona by identifying with positive qualities and repressing negative qualities into the shadow.

But to build the personality we need to live our shadows as well as our personas. We need to relate to all the opposites within and without.

What I consider positive is what I identify with. What I consider negative is what I repress and reject.

When I adopt a wholeness perspective, **I integrate the positive and negative, sacrificing only the extreme aspects of both. Integration is creating a new unity by including both opposites.**

Procedure

1. List the major roles you play in life. I am a ________________, etc. Which ones do you identify with? What are you doing to their opposites? For example, doctors may identify with being healers and project their wounded sides onto their patients, marriage partners and children. Mothers may identify with nurturing others, thus neglecting themselves and becoming overweight.

2. List the roles others see you in. List some images or roles which others do not see in you but which you might like to try out. Try them out in small little ways and see what happens.

3. Play with a role you feel you are over-identified with and play also with its opposite. "You be the mother now," you might say to your child. In ancient Rome slave and master used to change places and roles for ten days or so during the Saturnalia.

4. Create for yourself a meaningful role to operate from which you do not identify with. Let this role or self-image include expressing many different roles in life.

5. Welcome opportunities to operate in different ways from normal, like coming out of a movie theater and acting like one of the characters, or imitating someone's behavior which you either like (persona) or don't like (shadow).

To play many roles in life without identification with any contributes to wholeness.

6. Write up or meditate on the image of Life Journeyer as a new more comprehensive role and image for yourself which you do not identify with (inflation) but relate to (wholeness).

Example

A young man in therapy was having an awful time feeling guilty because he was not meeting parental expectations. He did not want to call his mother every week. He did not want to take his parents' money even though he was still in college. He did not like himself when he had sex with women, used them for mothering, and then left them to relate to someone else. He was to visit his parents on vacation soon and was dreading the experience.

"But all we have talked about here", I suggested, "is relevant surely in your home. If you want to get free of your parents you will have to act free. What is your name?"

"Jonathan," he replied. "Why?"
"And what do they call you?"
"Johnny."
"Do you see the connection?"

His eyes lit up and he worked out a plan with me. He would insist that his parents call him by his full adult name, and he would not call his mother "mom" anymore. He would use her human name of Rose.

Using real names is powerful medicine. If you find it impossible to do this for yourself then you will know the power of archetypal identification with a role, and the cost it has to the personality.

The end of the story?

The parents got upset about it at first but then went on to enjoy the name game. A new manhood emerged for him, one in which he could, among other things, work out of his dependency on mothering sexuality.

Disidentifying from roles is bound to lead to transformation and new life. We have choice in what roles and images we express.

Practice 10

INTEGRATING PROJECTIONS

"We project what we have not yet made conscious."

What hides reality from us? What stands behind so many of the most intense experiences in life? What must we learn to handle in order to deal with life? What must be understood to bring about transformation in this age?

Projection!

You are projecting. I am projecting. We are all projecting onto each other and onto situations.

"I may be projecting but I think that you . . . ." This would be a typical statement by someone developing new and ongoing consciousness. We can never be sure, can we, that what we think is out there is not really coming from inside ourselves?

Projection is experiencing as out there what is really within ourselves. We project everything we have not yet made conscious. We project the next growth step in consciousness. We project everything we do not know about ourselves.

The Major Projections in Our Lives

Since projection is putting out there what is really inside, it follows that the central dynamics of the psyche may be in projected form at various periods of our lives. We then look at what these dynamics are and how we can take back the projections and integrate the dynamics behind them into our lives and personalities.

The Love Projection

As C. G. Jung has quite simply put it, sex gets us involved in life. We grow up and want to mate, yet we are scared of life in the world and all its potent energies. If left to their own devices, many people might not even form the tight bonds which sexuality demands. There are warmth needs in a love relationship but there is also the major projection of one's opposite onto one's partner. **We seek relationship to find ourselves.** We want to mate with and experience our opposite. So the young men tend to identify with their genitals and the masculine and seek the opposite feminine outside themselves in a flesh and blood woman. If she responds, joy! One has found one's soul mate. If not, pure agony because a part of oneself has been projected onto another person who steals away, never to be seen again.

The agony of breakups is that we have strong projections onto our partners and other family members. When they disappear it feels as if they are taking a part of ourselves with them. And until we claim as our own the things they have carried for us, we will feel lost and split apart.

One secret to successful relating is to be integrating the projections onto each other as they become known. Then if the relationship splits you will have within yourself what has been evoked for you, and the loss will not be felt as overwhelming. **You have nothing to lose but yourself. You cannot lose another person.** You can give up your projections onto them by integrating them within yourself. We can turn image into function. If I think you are a wonderful dancer, I can learn to dance myself.

Another major aspect of the love projection, whether between lovers or family members, is that we tend to unconsciously try to fulfill someone else's projection onto us. We develop roles to evoke certain projections. We put on makeup and jewelry to evoke a feminine projection. We act in a bold and decisive manner to convey masculinity and to evoke the projection of strength onto us. We tend to identify with certain projections. We like the positive ones and identify with remarks of praise and love, while at the same time feeling uneasy, wondering whether they are talking about us or another person or even a fantasy.

We project the archetypes onto each other and try to get the other person to fulfill them for us. One way we do this is praise them when they act out our projections. The other way is to become angry and punishing when someone refuses to play a role and fulfill one of our cherished projections.

"You're such a happy person," we say to someone else. "I love being around you!" What a manipulation to get someone to fulfill a role for us! What if that person doesn't want to be happy all the time? What if they feel vulnerable and in pain? Where can they show that and be themselves? Nowhere with you unless you take back your projection and integrate it within yourself. Maybe you need to be more happy and playful? Develop that in yourself and let the other person be more what they want to be. Okay?

The Enemy Projection

Can you dash off a quick list of those you hate, absolutely despise, and so on? What? You don't hate anybody? Not even figures and events in the news? Where is your enemy projection? Where is your shadow expressing itself?

If we look again at relationship, what usually shoots holes in the positive love projections people put on each other is experiencing directly each other's shadow. What, you are not so wonderful after all? You shit and piss like the rest of us? You're selfish and unreliable sometimes? Oh, no! Is this the person I have chosen to live with? Is this the person who was going to be the answer to all my needs?

Everyone has a destructive and unintegrated side which they are uncomfortable with. What we don't like about ourselves we tend to repress. Repression causes both compulsion and projection. If we cannot face certain traits within ourselves we will project them onto others. Just as we saw our partners and friends as better than they are, we will now see them as worse than they are. They are receiving our shadow projection, and woe be to them if they cross us. This is what is called a love-hate relationship of intense proportions.

But we need relationship. We need to project onto people and work through our stuff. Unfortunately, using family and intimate relationships as conduits for projection causes so much unreality that people have to repress all over the place, and so you get things like family members not speaking to each other for months, or secret affairs on the side.

The amount of projecting evoked in relationship is so intense that many modern couples seek relationship counseling and individual therapy. They want to live together and relate, but they find it too hard to become complete therapists to each other. Like the realists they are becoming, they seek outside help.

Playing at War

The unsuccessful ones at developing an inner life often seek positions of power in business and politics. There in the political arena opponents can project their own neurotic selves onto each other and make impassioned speeches about the evils of the other side. Nation states project enemy onto each other and go to war in an attempt to annihilate the opponent. The opponent, the unintegrated side, is really inside oneself, projected out into the world. We project out there the evils we have within ourselves. War is an exercise in folly because the issues are unreal when acted out. Millions of people can be killed, and for what? Because they have projected their shadows, the enemy, onto each other and they seek the ultimate repression, annihilation and defeat of the opponent. It is reported that in a battle during the First World War a million men died in one day. This outrageous loss of life gets a single line in the history books, and what for? A million vital lives sacrificed to create one sentence which may be viewed by future generations as the ultimate barbarity. Had the world's people known about the shadow, this and other war atrocities might not have happened.

How much better, but how difficult, it is to integrate the shadow projection back within ourselves. It's more effective, less destructive, costs less, is more fun, gives greater health, aids freedom, and creates more harmony and meaning in life. How many jobs or other situations have you lost because someone projected the enemy onto you or you projected it onto them?

We can recognize a shadow projection by the feeling of internal raving, a heightened emotion of anger and tightness. We then ask, what am I projecting onto this person or situation which is really inside myself? And we write out whatever comes into our heads just as it occurs to us, censoring nothing. Then when we see that energy as being in us we seek ways to create with it. If I am all upset about someone pushing me around, then maybe I need to become more assertive myself. I do not just act the same way as my adversary, unless this is appropriate. I re-translate the dynamic into new forms for action and change.

In projection we project one opposite and identify with the other. If I hate dictatorial people out of proportion to the reality, then I have a secret dictator within which comes out compulsively when I lose control. Normally I see myself as an open, non-pushy person, but what I lose sight of is that if I identify with being soft I will not be able to become hard where appropriate. The creative and conscious way is to choose the energy we embody in the moment according to what is necessary in the situation. If we are identified with one side and repress the other, we will not have that choice.

Sounds like a lot of work? It is. But you don't have to do it. Maybe it's easier just to keep projecting onto those dirty commies, reactionaries, racists, revolutionaries, relatives, thieves, capitalists, men, women, doctors, victims, and so on and on. You could start today, or wait a year from now? So when you feel a heightened energy just let it rile you around inside or rant it out into the world. This earth is just a great big cesspool anyway and a little more of your shit won't hurt it. Go on! Don't take responsibility for your projections. If you don't know it by now, there is more than a little dark humor about projection and what it does to life.

The Authority Projection

We leave childhood physically not having fully dealt with the dynamics there. This means that we have projected both positive and negative qualities onto our parents and other authority figures. Who knows, maybe the ultimate parental projection is what many people call God, God the Father, or God the Mother, God the Source personified in the wonderful parent we never really had?

When we enter adult relationships we are going to project authority energy onto significant older people. These may be friends and lovers, bosses, teachers, doctors, political and entertainment figures. What we are projecting are still undeveloped parts of ourselves. I project parent because I have not yet developed sufficiently the parenting function inside myself. I may even be a good parent to my children, yet not to myself, may not foster my own development or satisfy my own needs. The parental function nurtures, structures, and protects new growth. The more I can take care of myself and act from inner sources of guidance, the less strong will be my projection of authority out onto others.

But we first project what we have not yet made conscious. It is so much easier, apparently, to see things as outside ourselves rather than within. So our goal is not to prevent projections, but to take them back and integrate them when they come up. You continually test reality. Why do I hate or love this person? How is that also inside myself? Is this really in that person, or am I projecting onto them? Usually, or always, there is a hook in the other person for our projections, and roles evoke projections. But if our reactions to a certain person or situation seem exaggerated we should check out the dynamics in reality.

Bring up the issue in conversation in an appropriate way. Maybe not, "I know I'm projecting all over you, but you are the most dynamic person I've ever met." Better might be, "Let's have lunch so we can talk together about our work. I would appreciate hearing more about how you have developed what you do, and I would appreciate any feedback you can give me about myself."

The Reality Projection

This is a hard one. We know from history that humans have projected all sorts of things into the sky and onto special events like solar eclipses. Kings and queens would receive enormous projections, and therefore power, from others. Today with television the image makes the person. The right image encourages the right projection, and people decide and vote according to their projections. If your television image encourages positive projections then you will be elected to office. But if your image and bearing encourages people to project shadow qualities from inside themselves, such as inadequacy, then you will lose the election. We project on others what we ourselves need. A weak and compliant people will project onto dynamic and decisive individuals. It matters far less what the content is, the leader must be the right image to evoke the right projection. And conversely, the more a people become assertive in their own right, the less they will project their own power onto dictatorial personalities.

How we see reality affects how we live life. If our strongest images of reality are those which come from advertising, for example buying a new car, then we will act as if buying a new car is reality. Where we put our time and money is in large part determined by our projections. The advertisers know this and give us images to make our projecting easy. Therefore when we buy some object out there we are really buying a part of ourselves. If we need to feel we are living new life we may buy a new car to symbolize this. This extraverting of the process keeps the culture going, but it also keeps the individual unconscious.

It is important to see what you are projecting onto the collective so that you may bring choice to it. Maybe I will stay with my old car and go into therapy instead to make changes in my life? A new car won't change my life, but being supported in my growth process will. Sure, I can change my hair style, my wardrobe, my friends, my address, but if I do not change my personality, what have I?

Take back your projections onto externals and you will be left with yourself. You have only yourself and how you perceive the world. That is all you have in life. Take back your projections and you will not be identified with the world and you can get on with the real work.

The Practice

1. First, begin the process of recognizing that you are projecting. Assume that you are projecting in every area of your life. Choose some issue or person toward whom you have intense positive or negative feelings now. Describe that person, listing all the qualities you see in him or her. Then what is the essence or root quality behind the rest? How are these root qualities unacknowledged or unexpressed parts of yourself? You can also check out with that person or others which of those qualities are really emerging ones in you more than being of the other person.

2. As part of your analysis when you get to the root qualities, evaluate whether they are opposites to dynamics you are identified with. State the opposites to the characteristics you see in the other person. How might you be identified with these? How might you develop their opposites within yourself?

3. Practice disidentifying from your identifications and projections by saying, "I am not this quality. It lives in me." Devise ways to express these dynamics appropriately as part of you.

4. We actualize the dynamics, whether positive or negative. by creating with them. If I love the way she dances, I will learn to dance. If he is outgoing and I am not, I will become more outgoing because I am attracted to his energy. Actually study your projectee and almost mime their style to experience a different kind of energy yourself. Practice and see what happens. Don't worry about copying someone else. You will develop your own way of expressing this energy. You must find it in yourself.

5. Integrate the dynamics you project. If you need to be more playful, be more playful. If a movie moved you, express that energy more in your life. Integrate both positive and negative appropriately. A flare-up of the enemy projection means that I am reacting against some dynamic I need to develop within myself. I have identified with one value and rejected its opposite. To live this way is to live only half of life, always in fear of the other half compulsively sneaking up on you and taking you over.

We take back and actualize our projections to arrive at the fullness of being which is our heritage.

Practice 11

TRANSFORMING ANGER

"The trick is to know how to express anger effectively and with a sense of choice."

We all get angry, whether we know it or not. Anger is such a fear-evoking emotion that many of us have learned to control and repress it. Controlling anger at certain stages is necessary, since otherwise it would break out into violence. At other stages letting anger rip can have a purifying and healing effect.

But anger itself often erupts in us, going beyond our power to bring choice to it, at least for awhile. The emotion is stronger than the ego, just as sex and love are at times stronger than the ego.

Our fundamental position is that anger expression is healthy and necessary in certain circumstances. We want no lovey-dovey saints here whom the world looks to as perfect because they seem to have no anger. Nothing could be farther from wholeness.

If you want to love, express hate. If you want to hate, express love.

The ego, as you know, identifies with the "good" side of the personality, the persona, and therefore rejects and represses the shadow side. But repression causes compulsion and projection, and sooner or later the shadow will burst forth, either as anger or as any of its sublimations.

Anger is often sublimated, or expressed indirectly, in passivity, exercise, games, smoking, drug and alcohol experiences, work, sickness, and sanctioned killing such as in war and policework. At a subtler level sublimated anger can come out as arrogance, saintliness, humility, manic and depressed states, and all sorts of bodily symptoms. While a certain amount of anger energy can be creatively sublimated, our basic approach is to express anger directly and work it through.

What is so bad about being angry? Here are some of the typical statements and attitudes in response to this question.

"People won't like me." —And why do you have to be liked?

"It's stupid to get angry." —Yes, it often feels that way, but what is so bad about feeling and acting stupid? Do you have to be smart all the time?

"I'm afraid I might hurt someone if I let go to my anger." —Why does anger have to mean hurting someone? There are alternate ways of expressing this violent emotion without destroying another person, even if you want to.

"I'm not in control when I'm angry. It just takes over." —And what is so bad about being out of control? What would happen to you?

"I just don't like getting angry. It's not a nice feeling." —And why do you have to experience only nice feelings? What's wrong with feeling terrible sometimes?

"It hurts." —Yes, anger does hurt. Don't you want to feel pain for the purification and change it can produce in you?

"I'm afraid to let my anger out. It might overwhelm me. I don't have the skills to process it in a way that doesn't take over my life." —Would you make a commitment to learning those skills so you can create with this great emotion?

"I destroy things when I become really angry. I don't like that." —Yes, anger is the emotion of destruction. What is so bad about destroying old ways, and even a few objects?

"I don't want to hurt other people." —What is so bad about hurting other people? It might even be good for them as well as for you. You're probably more afraid of being hurt yourself.

"I know my anger is inappropriate, It's really my mother I'm angry at, you just pushed my button. Why should I dump on you?" —You may have to dump mother stuff from time to time. Help your partner not to identify with it.

"Come on! You're quite a bullshitter, Strephon." —Try out this approach and see.

War And Repression

Why are we interested in anger transformation?

Wars are built on repression. The world's present crisis of violence is the inevitable outcome of our age-old approach to resolving differences, which is that each side tries to overwhelm the other. Both sides are defensive. Both sides try to stay rational until they see a strong enough advantage to enter into direct conflict. Then war vomits out.

The young do the fighting in wars while the old direct them. The young are just emerging from childhood with weak egos and much repressed anger at parents and others. The old, governed by their own repressions, skillfully direct that anger, guiding the young to project their own shadow side onto the enemy and then to righteously hate and kill.

Wars are built on repression. Only those who are full of repressed anger want to kill someone. Repressed anger makes us defensive, and so nation states use this defensive energy to fight their wars. If the leaders are full of repressed anger they will act defensively. They will be unwilling to make the compromises and changes in position which bring about reconciliation. Compulsively identified with their "good" persona, they will relentlessly seek to destroy the enemy, who carries their shadow projection. And they will as relentlessly seek to destroy any who threaten their identification with good. So internal opposition by those who would restrain their leaders' aggression may be as threatening to the leaders as an opposing nation-state, and leaders of peace movements, who are often themselves projecting their shadows onto the aggressive leader, find they are creating more levels of conflict.

The political symptoms of an age are really psychological symptoms as well, since all nations are made up of individuals, each with a personal psychology.

The Individual Level

Is there anyone who does not yet express anger fully in creative ways as it comes up?

Or are most of us still acting defensively with each other, afraid to get out our anger and our hurt?

Would you like to be free of your childhood repressions?

Would you like to be able to express all your emotions and feelings freely as they come up? Yes? Then are you willing to release anger freely as it comes up and work through the underlying issues to resolution? No? Why not?

"I want to express only the pleasurable emotions like caring, love and playfulness."

"Oh, so you want to be one-sided?"

"In your book that might be one-sided. In mine I call it healthy."

"So you think being healthy is expressing the positive and not the negative?"

"Oh shut up!"

"I will not shut up! Face reality."

"I don't want to."

The Process

We make a commitment to expressing and working our anger through to resolution whenever it arises. This is our basic commitment, and the outcome we receive from this process is the ability to respond at a feeling level to most if not all of life's situations in a direct and effective way.

People who are repressing or over-controlling their anger usually come across as shallow, one-sided, and judgmental. The judgmental people will often make glances or remarks which approve or disapprove of what we are doing. They will not express their feelings directly but will comment in general using some value system to evaluate our behavior.

The person expressing anger and feeling will not be that judgmental. He or she could care less whether what you did was right or wrong in some absolute sense. The feeling person either reacts positively or negatively to what you are doing from a personal point of view. Screw the abstractions. Let's get down to the specifics of what is going on between us. That is the feeling level.

If we fear intimacy and realness we will engage in all sorts of defensive measures in the moment to avoid the full and immediate impact of what is happening now. We will repress feelings, thus creating anger. **Anger is the emotion of repression.** How do we know this? Because when anger is expressed directly it always leads to underlying feelings of hurt, caring, love, enthusiasm, fear, and so on. The point for expressing anger is not to become some hotshot who is good at anger expression. Better to become a tennis star. **We express our anger to release the repressions underneath. We express anger to feel, to resolve the important issues of our lives as they come up daily.** Without feelings we do not know what our priorities are, we do not get in touch with what is really important to us so that we can let the rest go.

What is so bad about dealing with the real issues happening now?

So you don't feel loving today toward someone you normally love? Don't repress it. Share it. If the other person becomes angry and hurt then they are not loving themselves enough to handle when someone else does not respond lovingly to them. Honesty before repression whenever possible. **Repression is the universal lie, the untruth of truth.**

If there is something wrong with working to be totally honest with yourself and others, then do not work at freeing your anger up. Anger is real, and the feelings and issues being repressed are likewise real. **Anger is the non-acceptance of reality as it really is.** We don't like things not going our way so we repress their effects in us.

Anger is also a universal protest. Things should be other than they are. Some of my anger will be wanting things to be different and therefore attempting to resist things the way they are. All sorts of attitudes are continually challenged by what actually happens to us in life. We can have it no other way. Life is life as it is, not as we would want it to be. If we are angry all the time we may be protesting reality, we may have some attitudes and hopes for a different reality than the one we are heir to.

Anger as the Emotion of Protection

We are only ultimately angry with ourselves. This is a basic premise. If I am angry, then I have not protected myself in some way. If someone has hurt me or done something I didn't like, was I assuming that they would act any differently? Was I being naive and unprepared for the actual? So-and-so misses an appointment with me and I get angry. Was I so certain that she would show up that I made no alternate plans to use my time well? How naive can I get? Why do I continually hurt myself by not being prepared for any reality?

Most of us have grown up trying to repress the adversarial side of life instead of fully dealing with it. So we get upset and angry because things do not go our way. We get parking tickets or someone leaves us or we lose money or someone will not be warm with us. So What! Grow up! Accept the imperfections in life and protect yourself with creative alternatives for every situation. **Realism is the cure of many woes.**

Challenge—the Goal of Anger Expression

Many of us have emerged from childhood repressing our anger. We have tight and fearful personalities afraid to express who we are and how we feel. Then we grow, we work on ourselves, we become heavily involved in relationships. We open to other persons, we feel hurt, we may start to get angry, we may feel overwhelmed at times. We may go into therapy. In therapy or some other growth process we will work on our repressions and what we want out of life. Anger comes up for us more strongly. We may even become difficult to deal with. We may even lose a job or a relationship. But what then? What after anger expression? We move on to also express feelings and to take action on the issues of our lives.

We talk and act more freely, and we move from defensive personalities to expressive personalities. We also learn to transform anger into challenge, both of ourselves and others. **We learn to create with the energy of anger.** We do not go passive. We open up to situations. We become accepting of them. But we also enter into a good fight when necessary. Creative fighting means entering conflicts at a feeling level, expressing differences, making the situation real, and then both sides changing to create a new reality. **To be able to get what you want you must be willing to not get what you want.** But you must also be willing to really push for what you want. **You challenge a situation as well as accept it.** A person, then, in touch with anger is an effective person in life, able to both shift and be subtle and to be bold and cajole, depending on circumstances.

Will you be able to take being this full and vital a person?

The Anger Transformation Practice

1. First make a commitment to expressing your anger in some way whenever it comes up. No more repressing for you! This expression may take the form of direct confrontation with someone else, or of physical venting of emotion, such as car yelling (not car smashing) or pillow pounding, or it may be expressed in your journal or on a scrap of paper or in a letter you never send.

2. Develop an inner arena for expressing anger. All anger does not have to be vented out onto another person or situation. Write exactly how you feel in your journal. Write a letter in which you express your feelings fully, but you may or may not send the letter depending on how willing and able you and the other person are to deal with the reaction to it.

3. In processing your angry feelings, separate out what might be your projecting into a situation from what might really be the other person's stuff. To do this, first separate yourself from the content of the situation and focus on your feelings and your relationship with the other person. Do you feel, for example, all upset because the person is infringing on your rights? He or she is not playing fair? Or do you feel a deep hurt because you are not being acknowledged? Or do you have a vindictive urge to squash whoever is getting in your way?

Stay with the feelings and recall other times in your life when you have felt this way. Do you see a pattern emerging? What we project into the present may be symbolic of unresolved hurt from the past. If I have ungrounded fantasies about my love partner running out on me this may be a projection based on actual trauma from the past when a parent or lover did fail me.

Now remember yourself as a child with this feeling. Let an incident occur to you which caused you to feel this way. Experience yourself inside the incident. Who is evoking these feelings in you? Is it one of your parents? Is this a recurring kind of interaction with that parent? What was the usual outcome of such interactions? How did they mold your anger reactions?

Now imagine your present antagonist. Get a good image or feeling-sense of him or her. In what way is she like your former antagonist? An attitude? A personality trait? Or is it just the fact that he is in a position of authority? To the extent that you are reacting just as you would have reacted to your former antagonist, you are projecting and therefore behaving automatically.

Once you have separated out your own stuff, you can see the other person more realistically. No, he or she is not your jailor, your slavemaster, your betrayer. He's a person probably bringing as much projection to the situation as you are. You can recognize his by noticing his areas of extreme reactivity, rigidity, and irrationality. Don't try to confront them, don't try to make him be rational. Protect yourself and try to work realistically and creatively with the situation.

4. Have a dialogue with your inner parts. If you are angry with an outer person, first dialogue, write out your anger to that person and also write what that person responds back. Keep writing quickly until you feel a resolution leading to insight about the situation.

5. Always ask, what hurt is behind the anger I feel? How might I be in danger of losing something in this situation? Once you have found what you might be afraid of, then go on to express it in some effective way. You may not get what you want but you will feel better for having expressed what you want. **We do not have to get what we want if we can express what we want.**

6. Express your anger as direct feeling with your body involved. This might mean screaming into a pillow, or yelling when you are alone driving in your car. It might mean letting yourself tremble or dance out the energy in spontaneous movements. Pounding pillows may help express your angry energy if you then go on to express anger directly to those involved. Pillow pounding is no substitute for real life. Break things if you have to. But know that the final expression which leads to resolution is that of confronting your issues directly and resolving them through integration and action.

7. Express your anger until you get to your underlying feelings and issues. Express your feelings directly and then take action on your issues. Issues are the conflicts and potentials needing action and change in your life.

8. Develop honesty to the core. Do not let much slip by you by going unconscious. You must express more and more who you really are and not who you think others would like you to be. This expression of yourself can be done sensitively and decisively. You are the person living your own life. The more you live from your true self the less repressed anger you will have.

9. Write out your attitudes toward expressing anger and then write creative new ones which will help transform the old ones. Then write out a summary paragraph on the values of expressing anger and the practices you will use to transform anger. Transforming anger does not mean getting rid of it forever, but processing it through to the underlying issues in your life. Honesty, commitment and courage are required, and then we will have new vitality.

Anger Expression

Practice 12

DEALING WITH VIOLENCE

"Release the energy creatively and fear evaporates."

My earliest experiences of violence were when I would be beaten up by older boys in boarding school. How can I describe that feeling of helplessness when someone is beating on my body? I won some of my childhood fights, but others were disasters. I can remember pounding furiously on a stronger boy as he just held me, making me totally ineffective in my crying fury. At last at age fourteen in military school I gave up fighting. I got extremely angry at a classmate who was bugging me, and broke a clod of dirt over his head. For this he went after me and I was scared. To fight him I would have had to let go to my anger and hit out like a wild man. He kept punching me as I kept saying I did not want to fight. Then a man came by and broke it up.

My next fights were with women I was intimately bound up with. One of them loved our physical fights together. We were passionate in love-making and in our mutual violence, which was angry but never reached the bone-breaking stage. My worst period was with someone else whom I had to leave to get away from the terrible things we did to each other. Again, no bones were broken but there were slaps, even hitting, on both sides, bottles shattered on the floor, and one time my glasses were grabbed right off my face and crumpled up before my eyes. I believe I retaliated with my fist or a strong shove. I don't like to remember this stuff. That scene was too heavy for me and I left. Our therapists had tried to keep us together, which no therapist should do. I came to my senses and got out, saving both of us. It was a desperate situation for us and no salvation seemed possible.

My next friend I was much less violent with, and one time she herself kicked me lightly in the crotch with a flick of her toe when I was hassling her. I had also hit her one time when she wouldn't leave me alone. My violence had lessened but had not yet transformed itself. I needed something more and didn't realize it. Circumstances were shortly to come along which would teach me a big lesson about violence. Of course violence had been done to me often enough as I was growing up, and I had also had to repress my anger. What is especially vivid to me is my father holding me by my legs as a young child and tickling me, making me laugh. I hated being controlled in this way, and I could never get him to stop doing this parental violence to me. Now in the intimacy of adult relations the old anger and violence would come back up at desperate moments. I wanted to lash out, to smash my father for the way he controlled me and made me suffer.

One weekend when the stars were especially auspicacious according to the astrologers, I was visited with tremendous adversarial energy. I had been relating to one woman deeply but there were also difficult issues separating us. I had started another relationship while keeping my present one going. I needed, so I thought, to find the right woman for me. On a Friday night I was over at my new friend's house naked in the kitchen when a man I had never met but only heard about began breaking the wood and glass of her front door. It was of course her ex-boyfriend, who was sometimes crazy over her. Having gotten through the door he rushed down the hallway catching me as I was madly trying to get my pants on. His arm locked around my neck and I went after him as well, gradually forcing him to begin yielding. But my woman friend shouted at him to break up the fight, and he suddenly let go and dashed down the hall and out the door down the stairs never to be seen by me again.

I was dazed and amazed. Up until this point in adult life I had considered myself a gentle intellectual who drank good coffee, listened to classical music, and led a somewhat spiritual and psychological life. Here I had suddenly been brought low into the gutters of a common humanity. It was as if my most despised shadow had come in off the street to haunt me. There was power enough in dealing with two relationships, with each woman knowing about the other. Now external violence had entered the picture. She called the police. An officer came to make a report, and suggested that the only thing to do was "off" (kill) a guy like that. I was trembling.

The following night I was to spend with my other woman friend. Her former lover, who hated me, was again trying to relate to her. She was out somewhere with him when I arrived at the house where we had been living together. He phoned, telling me I had better be out of there when he arrived. I had experienced violence on Friday night and now on Saturday night I was again being visited with more of the Adversary. I was angry and fearful. I was not about to give up my territory. I went into the kitchen to get a long knife. This time I would defend myself. I locked all the windows and the door and waited. He had left without her and was heading my way. He wanted his things, she had called me and said, and I left them out on the porch. But I found a set of keys which I thought were his, and as I reached through the window to put them on the porch, he grabbed my arm. I jabbed with the knife and he let go. I shall never forget his crazed look at he tried to raise windows everywhere to get at me. I had called the police and finally they came and intervened, telling me to put the knife down, and then taking a report on him.

I had had my moment of glory in holding my own. Years later we talked and he said he had only been trying to scare me so that he could get back together with our mutual friend. I had been frightened. I honestly thought he would kill me, and I was prepared to kill if I had to. I had had enough of simply receiving violence directed my way. It was hard to sleep that night or to feel safe for many weeks following.

That much violence in one weekend drove me into training in the Japanese martial art, Aikido, which I still practice today. On the mat three times a week I express ritualized violence, first throwing my partner in various ways and then being thrown myself. I get tossed around almost daily on the mat and am aggressive with others. I have little violence left in me when I go home to my intimate relationships. I can become angry on occasion, but without the need to hit out and do direct damage.

Now I am becoming a warrior in the true sense of the word, one who practices the way of awareness and reconciliation of opposing forces in all things. I continually develop awareness, not only of myself but of all which surrounds me. I know the potentials for fear and violence and deal with them before they explode. I practice being ready at all times for the unexpected.

About a year ago I was tested in my ability to deal with violence when I attended a friend's wedding. During the celebration a band played country music and I, like everyone else, was laughing, dancing, and carrying on. But at the end a man came up to me saying I had better be careful. Someone was outside waiting to get me. His wife thought I had been laughing at him and had him all riled up.

What should I do? Confront the man directly to test out my Aikido techniques? Get angry that someone wants to do me violence and push me around? Sneak around the back way and run for my car to avoid a confrontation?

No, the best way was to gather a group of people around me and all go out together. He and his wife were there and stated their beef. He looked strong and tough but not overwhelming. If I were attacked and had to use Aikido I might just be able to handle him. But I simply said I was not laughing at him, that I liked the music and his dancing, and that I apologized if I had offended him in any way. Another man with me engaged him in friendly conversation and soon we walked on, and my friend and I drove off while I looked in my rearview mirror.

I had not lost or won the encounter. I had not stood up to him and told him he was full of shit and had better deal with his angry wife and not me. And I did not sneak away like a thief in the night. I had done the effective thing in the situation, which was to have a group of supportive people with me to prevent his irrational violence from erupting. I had practiced Aikido by avoiding a fight, yet maintaining a sense of focused awareness and self-composure.

My practice now is daily, even when not on the mat in Aikido. I try never to leave my awareness, even for a minute, anywhere in anything. Every sound has its message, and every nuance of conversation or behavior has some potential in it. I generally know now how people are interacting with me and I with them. I do not usually approach in fear and defensiveness, but in openness and commitment to blend with whatever energy might be coming my way. I never know what is going to happen, but then again, I do not need to know if I myself am in readiness for whatever potentiates the moment. **The game is played no matter the consequences. I do not play to win and I do not turn passive to lose.**

The principle is always to balance energy with energy, never striving to show superior force in a situation. If you have won in an encounter, you have lost just as much as if you had directly lost the encounter. **Harmony is the balancing of opposing forces so that a new way, different from each, can emerge.** I would not take the way of the policeman which was to simply kill off your opponent. Or the way of beating up women to get them to stop hassling me. Or the way of threatening to kill to effect a standstill. **The new way is not to match force with force of like character, but to balance force with different energy which makes possible resolution and new direction in life.**

Procedure

1. Write a history of your own violence, whether you are primarily the one who creates the violence or the one who receives it. What is the pattern and its transformation?

2. If you are either a victim or an aggressor how might you transform this role?

3. Practice open awareness of whatever is happening in each moment and also practice interacting in a blending, instead of a resisting manner, with whatever is coming your way.

4. Consider regular practice in some physical activity which will help you creatively release energy so that you do not have to repress it. Fear is awareness of repressed energy. Release the energy creatively and fear evaporates.

Practice 13

TRANSFORMING RELATIONSHIPS

"Relationship is growing separately together."

Relationship is growing separately together. We relate to others to find ourselves. We relate to ourselves in order to relate to others.

We work in the world and do other creative activity, but most of us seem more concerned about our intimate friendships. It is as if we cannot go through life alone. That would be too alienating. Yet we are born into the world single to ourselves and we die utterly alone. Nor can anyone else make our choices for us in this life. Yet most of us do not like to do things apart from others. We like company. We like support. We like help and advice in life's tasks. And well we might. It is difficult and one-sided to have to go it entirely solitary in life.

Yet in these modern times so many of us are having our view of relationship challenged. We may marry but then we will divorce. We may come together with someone in a great attraction of opposites, produce children, and then split apart because the two of us cannot live together since we have found out how little we have in common besides our children.

In the first marriage or major relationship we marry our parents. In our twenties we have left childhood physically, but mentally we are still trying to work through many of the unresolved problems originating in the biological family. I will find in you, my lover, the mother I never had. And I will find in you, my lover, the father I never had. We make a sexual connection and that becomes the biological connection all over again with the original family. The family archetype is evoked as we attempt to merge with each other.

Modern Relationships

The biggest issue in modern relationships is that we hang our dependency problems on each other and attempt to get the other person to live out parts of ourselves which we have not yet integrated. I will project my inner parents onto you, my relationship mate, rather than parent myself through life. You earn the living while I cook the food. If you play father to me I will play mother to you.

Yet relationships of this kind do not often survive into the middle years when people begin to seek consciousness of what is really happening in them. A whole new movement of conscious integration is occurring today.

For many of us it is no longer possible to simply merge with another person and project our opposites out onto them. We prefer to realize ourselves rather than manipulate and cajole, trying to get someone else we love to live half our lives for us. We have strong relationships but they are not the major focus in life.

The new way is to individuate, to see oneself as a journeyer through life who practices conscious integration. When I see that I am projecting a quality onto another person, I take it to mean that that same quality in myself needs to be cultivated and developed. So I *integrate* it into my own personality, I make it part of me rather than continuing to see it as "not me."

This means that even if I enter into a committed and fulltime relationship with you I will not let you depend on me to fulfill you, and I will resist your trying to parent me or in any way live my life for me. When we come together and meet intimately in deeply sharing ourselves with each other we will be taking responsibility together for who we are and what is evoked in our relationship.

The key to successful relating is to process alone and together whatever energies are evoked in the relationship.

In order to do this, **both members of the couple must be actively working on themselves and committed more to individual growth than even to the relationship.**

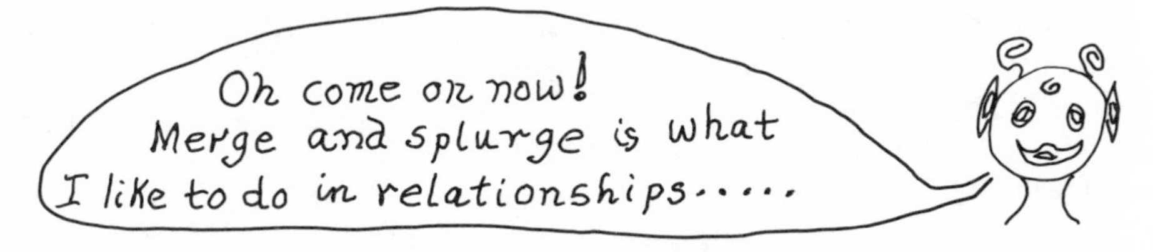

Oh come on now!
Merge and splurge is what
I like to do in relationships.....

In the past the ultimate commitment in life has been to the family archetype, to preserving the family and marriage at whatever cost to the individual. This has led to the celebration of fifty-year golden anniversaries. But few and far between have been the celebrations for those individuals who have realized themselves in withdrawing from the family archetype, even if they have stayed in their relationships.

The way of individuation is not the way of the family archetype. The family archetype, the preservation of the family and merger with it at all costs, is the death of individuation, of the individual realizing him- or herself in life. **The family archetype is projected wholeness, and individuation is integrated wholeness.**

Can one do both? Can one both have a fulfilling marriage and be able to develop oneself individually in all major aspects? If you learn how to deal with conflict creatively and how to live your life consciously, and you cease from being symbolically married to your parents, you may be able to do both.

This means differentiation as well as merging in your relationship. This means not hanging onto your children because they have become projected parts of yourself. This means not dominating your partner but letting him or her develop in their own way. This means a growing honesty and deeper communication between you. And it means making conscious and flexible the roles you carry out for each other. If she cries easily, learn to cry yourself. If he is good at making decisions, develop this ability for yourself.

Do not do things unconsciously for each other. Stop yourselves from creating mutual dependency. Then there can be the freedom both to relate and not to relate to each other. Sleep in separate rooms sometimes. Let each person have his or her own room, if at all possible. Be willing to fight and to challenge as well as to merge with and help each other. Create choice in all things in your relationship. You may be going through life together, and then again, you may not. If you are processing and integrating what you each evoke for the other you will not suffer as great a sense of loss should you at a later date part from each other to go your own separate ways.

The adult years are for the development of courageous personalities able to function independently and consciously in the world. Beware the strong pull back to the dependency of childhood which intimate relationships evoke. No wonder increasing numbers of people are genuinely afraid of marrying or living with someone. They do not want to become drowned in the dependency syndrome. If you must depend on someone and let go to your inner child, then hire a good therapist and work with him or her several years to resolve parent-child dynamics left over from childhood. Reliving childhood in adult relationships is natural but is not the goal in life. Do you really want to end up in your sixties calling each other Mom and Dad as your parents or your grandparents did?

Sex and Relationships

A man shares that he is not having enough sex with his girlfriend and he does not know what to do. He wants more sex and she does not want to give it.

Why define relationship problems in terms of the amount of sex you are having or not having? Why even go to a sex counselor for help? Why read all the books on sex? Or go after another lover?

First comes the sexual revolution. The genitals are liberated. It is no longer bad to have sex outside of marriage. It is no longer bad to engage in all sorts of sexual practices unless you are a fundamentalist religious person. We as a culture realized that the Victorian way was to repress the sexual function, even in marriage. The women were to be pure and not masturbate or swear or be sexually aggressive. The men were to keep their sexual indulgences hidden from public and wives' eyes. Sex was not a topic for public sharing. These attitudes meant repression of the sexual instinct and therefore of the emotional life. People lived in guilt and fear for engaging in animal behavior. They became so repressed that they tended to murder each other in wars and other outbreaks of violence and righteousness.

So today many of us have liberated our genitals. We enjoy sex. We like it with our friends and we like to try everything once. We may have many sexual partners in one lifetime. We may go nude together at free beaches and in hot tubs. We may joke about our sex lives. We may become good, uninhibited lovers who can really let go to our partners. We have achieved sexual liberation, but not necessarily liberation of our ability to feel and to relate.

For many people the most intense feelings in a relationship are the genital-evoked feeling states. Sexual expression may be the beginning step to liberating one's feelings, but a much more conscious attitude toward sex is required to move fully into relationships.

* You do not use sex to release tension, sexual or any other kind.
* You do not use sexual intercourse for masturbation by focusing on your own achieving of orgasm.
* You do not achieve sexual freshness in a relationship by trying new positions and fantasies.
* You do not give up on sexuality and the affectionate life because you have grown used to each other.
* You do not use the tremendous power of sex to manipulate others of either sex.
* You no longer see mutual orgasm as the major goal of love-making.
* You do not see the goal of courting as the achieving of a sexual liaison.

All of the above certainly are part of our sexual experience as well as such things as making babies. But what really is the basis for a fulfilling sex life?

The way to achieve sexual and relational intimacy in which the relationship continually freshens itself is to focus more on intimacy than sex.

"I don't like that about you. It scares me and makes me want to close off."

"That really moves me. I didn't know that about you. I guess I never cared enough to ask before."

When I reveal myself to someone else, I reveal myself to myself. There is little pretense or manipulation. We share of ourselves at honest and open levels. Relationship is shared vulnerability. In relationship we become increasingly vulnerable to each other by revealing more and more what we are, and this is intimacy.

Sex will always be fresh where intimacy is achieved.

When to End a Friendship

Relationship is growing separately together. I choose you to help me actualize my deepest self, and you choose me to help you become who you are meant to be.

Never keep a friendship any longer than the potential to teach each other something. Loyalty to another should never go beyond the evaporation of any purpose for being together. Holding onto old and worn out relationships takes time and energy away from developing new ones.

There is someone important about to enter my life and I must create space for this to happen now.

Say this statement a number of times to yourself and observe what it evokes for you.

What? You do not want to hurt anyone? You yourself would not want to be deserted by a friend?

Welcome every choice that someone makes not to be with you. This is an opportunity to be with yourself in your own creativity. Can you stand that, can you stand being alone with yourself? Or do you need people around you all the time to hide you from your own loneliness?

We are born single to ourselves and we die utterly alone as well. This is an unalterable law of life. Enjoy it. Live it. Do not seek relationships because you are needy and you yourself have nothing to give.

We welcome relationship to teach and to be taught. If you fail to meet a need of mine then I will have to meet that need myself, and this is a teaching.

We relate to others to relate to ourselves.

We need others to evoke parts of ourselves needing integration. We need others to project positive and negative dynamics onto, and then in the real life interaction we find that what we thought was the other person is really ourselves.

If you do not evoke new life for me then why should I relate to you?

Tradition? Past experiences? Family? Fairness? Obligation? Fear of being deserted myself? Myths, all of these! We will be deserted despite our best efforts to hang onto others. We will make choices which go against fairness, obligation and family because for each of us our own wholeness is more important.

I owe no one anything in this life. All debts for past services are cancelled from this moment onward. What you gave me then was your own reward. We gain in giving to others and lose in creating obligations from others. **Hold no one in your debt and they will then be free to give or not give to you.**

Then do I enter each relationship freely, actively letting go of the past. No, I do not know who will take care of me when I am old. I cannot and will not create this obligation now. How can we keep the future stable and controlled by the past? When I am old and dependent my usefulness on earth will be ended and I must exit. There is nothing more pathetic than someone or something which has outlived its usefulness. Throw the rug away when it no longer cushions the feet.

The Chief Purpose of Relationship Is to Effect Change

Review your attitudes about relationship in light of what has been stated. Are you trying to use relationship for unrealistic and immature ends? Look at your present relationships and determine what purpose you have for being together. If that purpose is no longer working, or if there is no real purpose, then end it by saying goodbye, and never look back.

We must always be ready for the new. There will be no lack of meaningful opportunities to relate if we are vital and alive to life.

You do not seek relationships. You seek life and relationship will come.

Yet when relationship comes we can choose to develop it further into its full potential.

And we do not simply leave a relationship seeking a better one. **Every relationship is preparation for the real one.** And the real one is what is happening now. **I learn to want what I have rather than wish for what I want.** I can learn to want the relationship I have until the relationship doesn't want me. This leads to realism in relationships and in life. There is no ideal lover or friend, just as there was no ideal parent in your childhood and there is no ideal God in your world view today.

No one likes to be around a loser. So then let us be winners. Let us be so in touch with ourselves that we are important and interesting to others. And let us be open and seeking so that others can find affirmation and purpose and teaching in being with us.

Have you as ego survived these last few pages on relationship? Write up and evaluate what has been evoked for you. You already have a set of attitudes regarding relationship. Some at least will have been stimulated by what you have just read. You can contrast and compare your own attitudes with what is presented here.

We are in relationship now. What do we have to teach each other?

The Practice

Think about the following questions. Write about them, and discuss them with others.Be aware of them as you pursue your relationships, and see how they affect your life.

1. What is your central goal in life? If it is having a primary relationship, then where does your own personal growth fit in? If it is to achieve your own wholeness, then where does relationship fit in?

2. What is your feeling picture of the primary relationship for you? Is this realistic? Have you achieved it, at least in part?

3. What compromises are you willing, and not willing, to make toward having a fulfilling relationship?

4. Describe your ideal partner. Then describe the kind of person you would need to be in order to relate to this partner.

5. What must you essentially have in a relationship in order to be able to relate? Have you achieved this yet?

6. How does your shadow side, your repressed and undeveloped side, affect your relationships? This is a big question, but begin to be aware of that side of yourself evoked in relationship which is inconsistent with your own wants and values. This too needs integration.

7. What makes you an interesting person to be with?

8. Relationship is growing separately together. Rewrite this in your own words. Find out what you really believe.

9. In summary, what are the five primary essentials necessary for you to have a fulfilling relationship?

An Example

I have worked with many couples during the last several years. Some of them stay together and some go their separate ways. I never consciously judge whether a couple should be together or not. Who is to tell? Who is arrogant and accurate enough to judge someone else's life?

Instead I encourage them to state their issues and I teach them how to communicate and struggle creatively.

I remember one couple who during a session had a terrible fight. But from there on over the next two months they gradually got so they liked each other again, and when they terminated counseling I could see that they genuinely enjoyed each other and wanted to live a transformed life in which they communicated and dealt with issues as they came up in their relationship.

The more magical part was that the man cured himself of alcoholism at the same time. He would bring his open bottle into our sessions in a brown bag. I never once referred to his bottle or his drinking and focused only on how they were and were not relating. I went with them down into their ultimate despair and rage and left them there, not knowing whether they would make it or not. I refused to interfere in one direction or another. My task was to help them unearth and express the suffering they had been repressing and which was making their relationship go colder and colder. I could not effect the transformation. I could only go with them to the nadir of despair, and where things are often most real, and train them in the skills for processing their material.

The transformation happened. They both saw the changes they each needed to make in the way they treated each other, and they made them. They had much left to teach each other and now they had ways to be effective in communicating and relating. They were about to have their first child.

THE FOUR FUNCTIONS

"We need each function
to be effective in life."

One of Jung's major formulations was his system of character types. He is responsible for creating the terms "introvert" and "extravert". The introvert is one whose focus is on the inward life more than the outer life. The introvert views life experience primarily by what it evokes within in terms of feelings, values, images, and other forms of inner experience. The extravert is outer-focused and finds more fulfillment in how people respond to him or her and what can be accomplished out there.

Most people have both their introverted and extraverted sides somewhat developed, while a minority are mainly one way and not the other. These extremes are expressed in shy personalities and boisterous ones, who never seem to get along with each other. In fact the basis for some personality conflicts lies in the unwillingness of people of different types to accept each others' differences.

Jung's other formulations on personality typology involve the four functions of Feeling, Intuition, Thinking and Sensation. We have each of these functions in us, some more developed than others. Our goal in working toward wholeness is to develop them all. We need each function to be effective in life.

We need our feeling function developed as the relational function. Feeling shows us what we like and dislike. Feeling is the energic function. All energy manifests in ourselves and in life as either positive or negative, as either outward moving or withdrawing.

We need our intuitive function to perceive the possibilities in life and the future. We need it also to give us direct insight into the core nature of an experience or person. We need intuition to develop creativity.

We need our thinking function to organize our thoughts, our feelings, our finances, other people, our life. Thinking discovers and develops the interrelations between things. We need thinking to make connections between past, present and future and to know what logically is possible. Thinking grounds creativity by organizing it.

In our exposition of the Jungian Personality Functions we note the possibility of eight types and not just four. This is because in many people the functions work in combination together. An intuitive thinker would be a theoretical scientist, while a sensation-thinker would be an engineer. A feeling-sensation person would love to touch people, and so on.

Most people develop one of the functions, or combinations of functions, as their dominant form out of which they make choices. They then tend to be weak in the opposite functions and seek others who might be good at what they are not good at, or sometimes reject others who are not effective in life in the way they are effective.

But working with the wholeness principle means gradually developing all the functions in ourselves. We all need to be organized (thinking), relational (feeling), practical (sensation), and perceptive (intuition).

In this book, developing each function becomes a transformative practice for the individual and the community or group. Organizations also emphasize certain functions and neglect others. In terms of the wholeness principle we would want all work places to be at once relational, organized, innovative and practical. And why not live your personal and family life in the same four-fold way?

Do not spend time on what your dominant function or functions might be. This is not a personality profile in which you can absolutely type yourself as being one functional type. Very few people are fixated in one function, or need to be. Not even a test such as the well-known *Myer-Briggs Type Indicator* can put you into a personality category. Tests often do not measure the personalities of the people taking the test so much as they indicate the personalities of the test designers. If you go to a baker he will give you a loaf of bread. If you go to a scientist you will be made into a statistic. If you go to a priest you will be seen as a sinner. **Go to your deepest self in this journey toward life and there you will find what you long for.**

Practice 14

DEVELOPING THE FEELING FUNCTION

"Better to express feelings than repress them."

For the full development of the human psyche, for the total functioning of our human abilities, and for the full experience of human life, we must have our feeling function activated. **Feelings are the inner experiences of energy expression, either positive or negative.**

"I feel rotten today."

"I'm excited! I can hardly wait!"

"I like it. I'm satisfied."

"I feel bad. I'm very upset about myself."

All of the above are good and necessary feelings to have, including the negative ones. Do not try and hide or get rid of your negative feelings. They are real and need acceptance and expression just like any positive feelings. In fact, the whole language of swearing is the language of repressed feeling. "Fuck you!" is an anger expression using a pleasure experience in a negative way. Repress your feelings, including your sexual feelings, and you will experience bursts of anger and swearing or, if not direct anger, then ulcers and righteousness.

Better to express feelings than repress them.

But there is a cost to practicing the above statement. To express feeling requires personal and emotional honesty. If you do not like something someone does to you, you need to confront them on it and let them know how you feel. But just because you have a strong feeling does not make you right. The other person may like exactly what you dislike. You can have differences and still express feelings. The goal is expression, not agreement or even compromise.

Feelings let us know where we stand, what we like and what we dislike, who we are and who we are not, whether we are fully living life or are half living it in a repressed state. **Repress feelings and you kill life.** Back in childhood we had to repress feelings, a form of lying which we all practiced in order to deceive the adult parents and teachers so that we could keep from being overwhelmed by them.

The danger in expressing feelings is that this will evoke strong feelings or emotions in others. You may lose your job if you feel intensely about an issue and tell your boss you don't like her or his approach. You may lose your relationship if you practice total honesty and tell your partner exactly how you feel about things. But you lose your affective life if you repress and don't express your feelings. If you are expressive, people will want to be around you even though sometimes you are quite negative, because you can also be quite positive about them and life. People become easily bored around the deadheads who repress themselves and do not show feeling.

Yet when we express ourselves fully at a feeling level the other person will be evoked. We must learn how to process whatever comes up. Anger, sexuality, depression, hurt, enthusiasm, inflation. These are powerful emotions evoked by expressing feelings.

What is Feeling?

Feeling is positive or negative energy expressed about some condition, event, or person. "I like" and "I dislike" are two common terms which are used to express feeling. Feelings are not emotions. Emotion is strong positive or negative affect which transcends immediate feelings of the moment. Grief and the love projection are two great emotions behind which are many feelings needing expressing. Grief carries with it a sense of loss, of loneliness, desertion, partialness, being overwhelmed, anger, feeling split apart, etc. To transform one's grief, break it down into its various feeling parts, express these and create new life with the energies. If you're lonely, seek new relationships. If you are sad, sing the blues, feel the hurt, and then let it go after it has purified you some more from your attachment to life. May you by the end of your long journey not grieve your going because by then you have lost your attachment to everything in life.

In relationship usually one person is more expressive of feeling than the other. It always happens this way. Two high energy feeling types could not stand to be with each other as much as couples are. And two low feeling types would become cold and stiff living in each other's presence. The feeling expressive type is drawn to getting the other person to feel more and to being structured and contained by the person who feels less. The non-expressive person is drawn to the highly expressive, both to contain what looks like fires raging and to be stimulated to more expression of what they seem to lack in themselves. The danger in such a relationship is that the feeling type will dominate with feelings and the less feeling person will ride on the other person instead of having feelings of his own.

In my own behavior I seem more to respond to others' feelings than to have ones of my own. I must resist being taken over by someone else's feelings until I can get to how I feel and what I want in a situation. I may be good at thinking and creative ideas and insights, but I sure miss a lot of the directness of relationship when I am not in touch with my feelings, as my friends know. I must then work consciously at developing feeling because it is not my natural gift.

People who are strongly expressive of feeling have their own problems. And the rest of us may have problems with them from time to time. Feeling types may well be called "crisis personalities" since these intense expressers of feeling often make it seem to others, and even to themselves, as if the world is coming to an end.

If you are a feeling type you will know this because of how you relate to crises and other kinds of change. It's as if everything is imagined a hundredfold. You hardly know if you will survive the event. You may cry, take to your bed, call people up, tremble, lose your breath, feel your head spinning or expanding, have sores break out on your mouth, pant, and so forth. You are in a tizzy and don't know how to get out of it. But you always have a friend who doesn't strongly react to you but helps you sort things through. He or she may be a thinking type, one good at organizing and abstracting experience.

Your goal when you feel is to also think. And when you think to still feel. Feeling types can fall into extremes with their thinking. This could take the form of head-spinning and headaches. Too many thoughts keep going around inside your head and you don't know what to do. Thinking says organize and feeling says act. The way to think is to think-feel. Feeling will tell you what is most important and real, and thinking will help you break your actions down into achievable steps towards the solution to your problem.

The Practices for Developing and Expressing Feeling

In the exercises which follow we need to stay aware of the distinction between feeling and emotion. Expressing emotions all over the place can be overwhelming, such as expressing anger whenever and wherever you feel like it. All emotions should be broken down into feelings, which are the specific reactions to things. When I'm angry I feel hurt, frustrated, upset, scared, powerful, all at once about specific things going on in me and my life. I differentiate my anger and express the feelings appropriately. I try not to express the emotion inappropriately or all balled up in a knot.

1. As the first exercise, take a recent emotional experience of your own and break it down into all the specific feelings which might have been involved. Each feeling will be positive or negative, have an attitude behind it, cause a bodily reaction, express a psychological state in energy and image, and have a specific object, event or action as a focus. Some of the causes of the emotion and its attendant feelings will come from the present and some from the repressed past. Include both. Then describe also the appropriate expression for each feeling. Feelings motivate actions.

2. Express yourself, even if it comes out crudely. Keep expressing and things will become clearer. If you cannot come up with a direct like or dislike, then come up with a spontaneous image of how you feel. "I feel like a rotten egg." "Well, how does a rotten egg feel?" "Just awful. I've goofed. I'm fragile. I feel like I'm not good for anything." Express yourself with courage and commitment. Risk more and more in saying exactly how you feel. Do not try to be responsible for how the other person reacts to your feelings. That is their problem. Trust that they will deal with it.

3. Always express feelings in the first person. "I feel shitty." Not, "You stupid shit."

"But I feel he is a stupid shit," you say.

"Yes, but how does that make you feel? Who cares what the other person is, or how she or he acts."

Turn judgments into feelings by making You-statements into I-statements. When you make You-judgments you put the other person on the defensive. When you express I-statements you give the other person feedback about their effect on you. They will be more able and willing to change as a result.

4. Never criticize or praise the whole person. This is judgmental, and you are setting yourself up as an evaluator of another human being. "I think you're wonderful!" is just as judgmental and damaging as saying "You're a stupid asshole!" In truth we are many things to many people and to ourselves. We do not need to identify with the good or bad which comes our way. If you identify with praise you will identify with criticism. Why not be free of both? We can express positive and negative feelings about a person's actions and still communicate effectively. "I like the way you did that." Or, "Your dirty underwear turns me off." "Why does it turn you off?" "Good question. I don't know why. It just does." Which says that we do not need reasons for how we feel in order to act on how we feel.

5. Do not let anyone talk you out of how you feel. They may ask for reasons or even tell you you shouldn't feel a certain way. That is none of their business. Ask them to express how they feel about your feelings, what effect are they having on them? Let them know that you do not like their criticizing your feelings.

6. Investigate for yourself how you feel. There may be attitudes behind your feelings. If you have the attitude that people should not express tears in public, you may well feel upset when this happens. You are entitled to your feelings, but you can also change your attitude so that you can feel something else when someone close to you cries in public.

7. How is sex tied up with your feeling function? How do you use sex to express feeling? What kinds of feelings do you express or repress when engaged in sex? How can you use sex to open up your feelings more?

8. What is a feeling for you? How might you express your feelings even better than you are now doing? If you don't know what you really feel about something, look for an image inside yourself and go from there. Also become aware of your body in the situation and this will help you get to what you are feeling.

9. How do you feel about this chapter? What attitudes and issues are behind how you feel?

Practice 15

USING YOUR INTUITION

"You have to be willing to be wrong to risk being right."

We have all had the experience of knowing we should have acted a certain way but didn't, and then the results were not to our liking. But if we had only followed our intuition, we say to ourselves, everything would have turned out well.

Intuition, according to C. G. Jung, **is direct perception through the unconscious.** I like to define intuition as a **direct perception of potentials.** We are able to see the possible before it is a concrete reality. We know what could happen if only we make certain choices. But most of us are afraid to risk, to step into the unknown from the known. We instinctively know what to do, but it is so different from what our rational mind is telling us that we do not do it, and we regret the outcome later.

"I should have married Charlene instead of Beth. But I didn't. I married the sensible one and I feel miserable."

"I had a feeling things would go wrong there, but instead I just went along with your saying everything would work out fine. I didn't check things out for myself, and now look at the mess we're in."

"I can't explain it to you yet, but if we follow this way of proceeding I think we will get better results. Trust me. Have I ever been entirely wrong before?"

"No, but there is always a first time," you might say to the person practicing their intuition above. Intuitive leaps are not always right. How difficult it is to separate out one's projections of what one wants to happen from what can really happen. We risk being wrong as well as right.

What intuition is good for is break-throughs. When the creative process seems totally blocked for you, use intuition. Listen inside yourself for the most unusual idea possible and mentally pursue it all the way into the future.

To open oneself to one's intuition is to open oneself to one's unconscious, that vast reservoir of potentials. Quite possibly the Self itself,theCentral Archetype of personal destiny and wholeness, speaks to us and would guide us using the crystalline voice of intuition, that inherent knowing which precedes conscious reasoning, and gives us awareness at the deepest of levels about what can happen in a situation.

Central to coping with life effectively is using all of one's powers to the maximum. We are given major crises to deal with in life, and we have the potential to deal with them, if we can but recognize our power and actualize it. Intuition is the guide to the best and only real direction to go in situations. Not to use intuition is to limit oneself to the known instead of learning to bring potential out of the unknown.

Example—Avoiding Disaster

This real life situation was reported to me by one of my students. She was living in Colombia at the time and woke with a dream of her daughter's bus being blown up. It was on a school day, but this mother had such a strong intuition about her dream that she would not let her daughter take the bus that day. Someone had planted a land mine in the road and the bus the daughter would have been on blew up causing the deaths of some of her friends.

The lesson is dramatic. **You have to be willing to be wrong to risk being right.** Some dreams will represent inner disasters and not outer ones. In this case the mother had an intuitive certainty about the dream and followed it. Using intuition gives us an edge in life for dealing with the unknown.

Intuition Expresses Itself in Two Ways

A person with **unconscious intuition** has all sorts of bright ideas on almost every subject. They have a million projects they would like to do and hate missing out on any potential. Because this intuition is unconscious it has a compulsive quality. Intuitives of this type start many projects and finish none of them. They even enjoy the way they are and take little responsibility for their creative insights and ideas.

Conscious intuition, by contrast, is direct perception of what is most essential. Instead of entertaining many grand ideas about what one could create, use intuition to discover the most essential or key potential to develop out of them all. This is conscious intuition involving a committed awareness and choice-making ability.

The Practice

1. SLOW DOWN. To hear the voice of intuition you have to "unbusy" your mind. Sort out your issues, yes, but also let your mind go blank and see what feelings, ideas, and images spontaneously emerge. In these is your intuition.

2. When a sudden perception or creative idea comes into consciousness, check it out. What is the opposite of the idea? Do I feel a special certainty about it? Do I resist it, therefore it must be right? Does it really express what may be a breakthrough solution? Am I intrigued by it? Is it possible for me to accomplish in reality? Have I generally been right in this area before?

3. Sort through your intuitions and bright ideas and decide which are the most essential ones and the ones that you can actualize in reality. Make a value tree if you have too many possibilities in life. Write twenty keys words for the potentials you see possible in your life at this time. Then using intuition, which five seem most essential or valuable to you? Then using **conscious intuition**, sort out the one or two central possibilities which are most realizable at the present time. Choose these and do them, using sensation as the practical function which gets things into concrete reality. Will you commit yourself to doing the work required, and not jump to other intuitive possibilities when the going gets rough or slowed down?

4. Practice living more fully by saying whatever comes into your head and doing whatever your intuition suggests. Thinking, the rational mind, says do only what is appropriate and reasonable. Intuition says do the somewhat wild and impossible. It might just work and open up a whole new avenue of reality.

Practice 16

OBJECTIFYING LIFE THROUGH THINKING

"Thinking organizes our experience according to innate relations between things."

Objectivity is seeing life and reality as they are, an impossible task in one sense, since we are always biased. What we think a situation is like may really be one large projection of unconscious contents. Am I dreaming or is this real? Will I stub my toe on reality today?

Thinking is the function within our psyches which perceives the inherent relations between things. If I do not add up the figures in my checkbook there is an almost certainty that I will overdraw my checking account. If I keep doing mean things to my lover, my lover may leave me. Thinking organizes the many facets of our experience according to innate relations between things. Logical thinking means taking a process through step by step, based on the way things are actually interrelated.

We use thinking to objectify our situation in order to gain the overall picture within which our own egos with their wants and desires are only a part. To see the world from an egocentric point of view is to subjectively interpret reality. To be interested not in what is, but in what I would like things to be.

Most business situations emphasize thinking over feeling, its opposite. When there is a job to be done within a specific time limit you cannot spend half the day being upset over how the boss is treating you. You have a goal to accomplish, and going into feeling will inhibit your ability to make immediate progress. On the other hand, if you have to repress your feelings, your thinking will not work well either. For you will be using thinking to repress feeling, and the repressed feelings will take energy away from accomplishing goals. So even though you have a thinking job to do, try and take a few minutes to be relational with those you work with. And in feeling situations, such as home life, do not give up on thinking. Organize your time there as well, so that you can express feeling in a way which will not take over everything you might want to do on a weekend.

Actually, the functions do not work in isolation from each other. In business thinking is required to keep focused on and realize the goal, such as a 20% increase in sales. But sensation is combined with thinking because most business goals are numerically defined. Accounting is sensation-thinking. The details are focused on and organized. The feeling function is used in business in improving morale and motivation, using both the negative energy of fear of being fired and the positive energy of enthusiasm for greater success for the company and promotion for oneself. Intuition is needed in making forecasts for the future, determining the trends, and creating new products which meet new needs in society. Entrepreneurs are strong on intuition. They innovate. Executives need to be strong on thinking-sensation. They organize and ground the organization in the practicality of its details.

The Practice

1. In order to develop thinking, devise ways of further organizing your life. Make plans for the year in certain areas. Make plans for each day, each week and each project you commit yourself to. Thinking organizes reality.

2. In what ways is the thinking function expressed in your life? Some people read mystery novels, they like unraveling the plots. Others do puzzles. Wherever thinking is required in your life, do it. Do you neglect certain areas such as personal finances? Perhaps you need to obtain help in keeping on top of these?

3. To feed the thinking function so that it does not try to outdo or take over the feeling function, read serious material such as philosophy, psychology, religion and science. This can be a pleasure from time to time, since you are using your thinking for other than just the everyday necessary tasks. If you do not feed your thinking function it will take over in head-spinning, anxiety, incessant mulling over problems and believing in unrealistic philosophies and opinions. If you do not think for yourself others will think for you, will tell you what to believe in life.

Practice 17

GROUNDING YOURSELF WITH AN ACTIVE SENSATION FUNCTION

"A developed sensation function means being in tune with concrete reality."

In a dream the dreamer was being told by a friend how to get grounded. She was instructed to attend to the practical details of life, for example, to put the soap back in the soap dish after use. The dreamer began sensing her feet in touch with the ground as she walked. Later in her waking life she started practicing this dream advice and things seemed more immediately distinct and colors brighter.

Many of us are not all that organized except where we have to be,in job situations and doing taxes. Using one's sensation function means paying attention to relevant details and organizing the placement and timing of things in a practical way. We are much more effective in life when we stay organized. If you cannot handle the sensation details of your life and feel overwhelmed by them, seek help from someone with a knack for ordering and getting things done. Each of us is responsible for continually processing the innumerable details of life. **A developed sensation function means being in tune with concrete reality.**

We may be sensual. We like to eat, exercise and make love. These are sensation-feeling experiences which help get us out of our mind, our thinking and intuitive powers. But in order to actualize potentials discovered by intuition we must attend to the details. Sensation is a slower process than intuition, and so intuitives can easily become impatient when they have to be practical.

The Practice

1. When doing a concrete sensation task, focus on the experience in itself. Get into the details and feel of the thing. Relish the obvious. Slow down and become physical.

2. Go through areas of your life and organize. You may need help in doing this. It is easier for us to organize others than ourselves. Clean off that desk by letting go of old stuff and sorting the rest. Organize. Pay attention to the details of your life. Clean out the refrigerator. Make a detailed plan of some project needing accomplishing.

3. Practice bringing resolution to the details of life each day. Do not leave dirty dishes overnight. Throw stuff away each day. Sort out your desk daily. Make lists of all you need to accomplish in a day. Relish the details!

Practice 18

RELATING TO SOURCE THROUGH ACTIVE IMAGING

"Strong imagery often happens because some new energy is moving in our psyches."

Breakthroughs in personality development occur through releasing blocked or undifferentiated energy. In the normal course of living we establish set patterns within ourselves of who we are and how we are to approach life. Some of these patterns are defensive. We block out the unknown and the fluidity of potential it would bring. Much of our defensiveness is originally formed during periods of trauma and stress. We repress the painful, but in repressing we push down and cover over vital aspects of ourselves.

Active imaging is one primary way to unlock the vital energy of the personality so that new life may develop. **Imagery is the royal road to the unconscious.** Images are the natural products of the patterns within, the archetypes. Through evoking and working with our imagery experience we approach the unconscious at its core and use that energy creatively for new life.

I prefer the phrase "active imaging" to the traditional Jungian term "active imagination" when it is used to describe the conscious use of images the way artists or visualization practitioners do the process. **Active imaging as used here means opening oneself up actively to source energies in the unconscious and seeing what happens.** We do not create or even suggest the image. We let it happen to us and then interact with it. This is active imaging.

One person has a dream in which a goddess figure appears before her in a dangerous and overwhelming way. The unconscious gives her the imagery, she gives herself the task to relate to that imagery and see what develops. In a meditative state she again sees the imagery of the dream and has a dialogue with the goddess. She is led somewhere new and the goddess changes shape.

Or I have seen a movie which powerfully affects me. I cannot shake the last scene and I go home to nightmares. What am I to do? Using active imaging I let go to the imagery experience completely and go through it until some kind of resolution occurs. Perhaps I place myself in the scene and fight the adversary there? Or I let myself be overcome by the dark forces and feel what that is like. I do whatever is necessary to bring resolution to the experience, even though I do not know in advance what that resolution will be.

Active Imaging Contrasted with Visualization

Active imaging is a process in which we open ourselves up to Source on the image and feeling level. It is not guided visualization or a form of dream control. We do not seek to produce a certain imagery, as an artist might. We let go to the imagery-producing function and allow things to happen.

Dream control, or lucid dreaming, is a practice in which people seek to control the kinds of dreams they have and what kind of imagery is produced. Guided visualization techniques have much the same approach. Active imaging is not a method whereby you visualize yourself in a beautiful meadow in order to relax. If you want to relax using active imaging you go into a meditative state with your eyes closed, let go to whatever imagery wants to be there, and follow that through until either it becomes too scary or you feel a sense of resolution develop. Bringing resolution to tensions is the most relaxing technique of all.

This is not positive thinking in imagery. Some consciousness teachers suggest that if you visualize what you want in life you will more likely get it. Here, by contrast, the ego is asked to purify itself by not attempting to get what it wants but by **letting go to what the source wants.** Whatever comes up is what you deal with. Even if the imagery seems overwhelming, you interact with it with intent to bring healing. In your active imaging you can be active as an inner ego function interacting with other characters and situations, but do not attempt to control the outcome by visualizing good things happening. Let happen whatever your psyche wants to happen. **You are not controlling your psyche but relating to it.** Trust that whatever happens is real and the real is what you deal with. If you need outside help, get it. But do not deny the reality of the dark side or its potential for healing.

The danger of controlling your visualizations is that you will make the ego reign supreme and will thus lose any chance to receive spontaneous material from your non-ego sources. You contaminate the psyche by trying to control it.

Should We Act Out or Contain Our Fantasies?

Within the Jungian approach are a number of introverted techniques such as dialoguing with images or painting them. You may also meditate on the images or allow them to continue and develop until resolution occurs. Usually, strong imagery happens because some new energy is moving in our psyches. We can let ourselves experience this energy as it comes up, even if it involves behavior we would never do in outer life. If you find violence or sexual material surfacing in your active imaging, let it. The inner world has its own rules and needs the energy brought into consciousness.

Most anti-social behavior is compulsive, the result of being locked into an inner pattern. This locked pattern shows up in imagery, even though we are in control enough not to act it out. We may have a fantasy which we repeat over and over to ourselves. The goal is to unlock this pattern by going through the imagery fully to resolution on the inner level. Acting out inner material may make it more alive to us, but does not in itself free the energy behind the fantasy so that we may have new life. Dialoguing with a fantasy figure also helps make the process conscious. Active imaging as a method is both talking with an image, not imaginary, figure and interacting with that figure in some meaningful way. Images from within which spontaneously appear are real because they manifest inner parts of ourselves. Imaginary figures, however, can be created by the ego just as concepts are created. At the least, these creations will be partial descriptions of personality dynamics. At the most they will be borrowing from sources outside ourselves and not really natural to our own development.

If you are frightened by the imagery experience this is healthy. Fear is a real feeling and not to be denied or changed. Feel the fear and go through it. If you cannot, some teachers suggest bringing in positive figures and objects to deal with the adversarial forces which scare you. This may have some value but we take a different position here. Any imagery which comes up is of the source and therefore potentially healing when worked with and followed to resolution. If you are being killed in a dream, go through it. Do not make it into a "good" dream. If you want to do some outrageous behavior in the inner world, do it, to release the energy so that you may integrate more sides of yourself into your conscious life.

If, however, you are feeling overwhelmed, or sense that too much is happening, stop, and ground yourself doing everyday things. Do not unleash your unconscious all at once. Some people experience dizziness and lose a sense of who they are as personalities and bodies. The ego boundaries seem to go because of the intense energy. So take the process in small doses that you can integrate. Seek professional help if you feel a loss of control, or if the inner life is overwhelming the outer life so much that you sometimes cannot tell which is which.

The Grounding Visualization

For those having intense imagery experiences with physical symptoms, some variation of this grounding exercise is recommended.

First, with your eyes closed and yourself in a sitting position, stay with the imagery and bring it down to size, a size you feel you can handle. Also see yourself in the picture in balance with what is happening. Then bring the experience itself into your body. Bring your awareness to your body. Lower it from your head, or above your head, down into your heart and guts. At the same time sense your grounding on the earth. Feel where you are sitting or standing and accept energy from the earth. Become as solid as possible in your own organicity, the guts, the blood, the sexual organs, the belly, the bones, the heart. You are an individual journeyer on this earth. Focus your energy. Now look for or allow to crystallize within yourself a healing presence or object. Follow your breathing as you see the essence of your being forming. Be still and focused with this center within for as long as it takes to get back inside your known self. You may repeat your name a number of times.

You may also repeat a healing saying, such as, "Healing hands hold and heal me . . . healing hands hold and heal me . . . ." When you have grounded and the symptoms are gone, slowly open your eyes and look around at your everyday reality. Still stay with your feelings and do not try to do outer things right away or talk much. If you do not feel a sense of grounding and resolution from this exercise then do whatever you have to do to put yourself back into everyday reality and your identity. Don't push a process farther than the point of integration for the material. If you are evoking more than you can process, stop!

I have always been able to bring people back from intense active imaging experiences with this technique. The unconscious is powerful and potentially overwhelming. It also has the source for new life. Our practice is to work with this energy, releasing only as much as we can integrate through conscious living. How much is released each session depends on what the person allows and what the psyche wants to give. Some people approach afraid and cautious. Others approach innocently over-yielding, or too rational. The conscious approach is to enter the meditative state purposefully letting go, with the overall commitment to process whatever comes up.

Some Principles Involved

* **Go into and through the darkness for healing.**
* **We do not seek control but maintain individual presence. We interact and relate with full being.**
* **The Source needs consciousness to be actualized.**
* **There is little vitality in the rational mind alone.**
* **The journey means both letting go and integrating whatever comes up.**
* **Evoke and process what is evoked.**
* **The negative is as positive as the positive is negative. They are one whole.**
* **To get where we are going we must allow a coming.**
* **The source has the potentials. We give choice to the process.**
* **The goals of the inner world are to bring resolution and to create new life.**
* **Through imagery we approach the source.**

The Practices

1. When you feel blocked in any area of life take a few moments, sit down and relax into your breathing, close your eyes, and to the best of your ability open up an inner space for yourself. With your issue in mind let any imagery come into your awareness and follow it wherever it wants to go. Your task is to follow and at some point see yourself interacting with what is happening. You may choose to dialogue directly with a figure which comes in. Do not try to control or make certain imagery happen. If you cannot let go of the tendency to control then let go to the controlling tendency and let that happen. Keep moving with the imagery until a sense of resolution develops. You will feel the energy change, end, resolve. It will feel like a new possibility or natural conclusion. Insight and new direction will have been gained. The authenticity of the experience usually depends on whether you have let go enough so that what happens is really new and unexpected. Then when things feel fairly complete, open your eyes and reflect on or write about what has happened for you. If you start feeling overwhelmed, do the grounding experience described earlier.

2. Use active imaging, and what we call dream reentry, with a vivid dream you have had. Choose your main scene and an intention, go into a meditative state, then re-experience the dream again as it was and then as it further evolves.

3. Take one of your standard fantasies which you seem to have over and over again. It may be sexual or violent or inflated. Usually locked within the images is new potential not yet realized. Let yourself in a meditative state fully experience the fantasy without censoring. Let new imagery come up, or interact more with the material. Then reflect on your experience and explore how you can better integrate the energy into your everyday world. **Turn image into function.** Commit yourself to do what you do in fantasy, but in an appropriate way. Fantasy sexual aggression can symbolize the need to be more expressive of feeling or the need to socialize more, go to dances, meet new friends, etc. Your fantasy will lose its energy as fantasy when you successfully actualize what it symbolizes in everyday life.

4. Develop for yourself a number of symbols, figures and objects, which symbolize different parts of your psyche. Dialogue with any of these when the time seems important or relevant to a particular character. These are your guides. Include dark as well as light ones. Do not worship the light and avoid the darkness. That genie in the white bottle is both a demon and a friend.

Practice 19

USING DREAMWORK

"We dream to wake to life."

Dreams are a gateway to the soul. If we never open the gate through dreamwork, will we ever arrive at union with that most essential part of ourselves?

Dreams, the windows that open upon the night, murmuring all our inner dynamics and needs for wholeness. Having worked now with thousands of dreams, including many of my own, I have found that most dreams are unresolved, that most dreams need healing, need our conscious awareness and devotion.

It is as if the dream source, the originator of the dream, is a self-regulating function within the psyche which presents to us the unresolved issues of our lives and the potential resources for dealing with these issues. We have only to make the problems and potentials conscious and choose to actualize resolution for healing to occur.

And out of every resolution life principles become known.

Example

One person becomes conscious while dreaming and has a series of dreams in which she realizes she is dreaming and changes the scene. She creates sexual outcomes for what she is dealing with, but she wakes disgusted at what she has created. I suggest that she can let go to the experience instead of control it and the following night she has a dream in which she is swimming far out at sea, becoming weak and close to going under. She remembers that I told her to let go and maybe a natural healing force would respond. She lets go to the ocean, stops desperately trying to make it, and is carried ashore by the waves. She walks up the beach, to the amazement of her friends. After this crucial dream she has no more lucid dreams. She misses that ability, but she has undergone a life change. She has a new life principle by which to live.

When I let go of trying to control life, life can respond with healing and transformation.

And said again,

When I let go to my soul, my soul knows what to do.

Example

Another dreamer, after years of working with her journey and her dreams, has the best dream of her life. She has often had dreams in which the ground opens up in front of her, or buildings collapse, or she feels greatly hassled and intruded upon. Now in this new and wonderful dream she enters her old house and finds it is intensely new, with beautiful rooms. From the upper floor windows look out on all sides with beautiful vistas, mountains and valleys in great clarity. She has worked long and hard and now experiences an amazing possibility for new life. She makes major new life choices which turn out well.

Life can be full and expansive if I do not allow myself to get caught in anxiety and inadequacy.

Ongoing wholeness is possible for anyone willing to pay the price of becoming conscious.

When we remember and work with at least some of our dreams we are using a third of our life—the creative sleep time—to bring renewal and direction. **We dream to wake to life.** Why waste a third of one's life through unconsciousness?

There is available now a full methodology for working with dreams which you can use on your own, with a therapist, in a dream group, or with a dream partner. We have developed the approach based on Jungian psychology and certain dreamwork concepts and practices attributed to the Senoi people of Malaysia, the so-called "dream people" who used their dreams for personal and community healing. This approach is available in our workshops and in the companion volume to this book, the *Jungian-Senoi Dreamwork Manual.* This dreamwork manual is designed to be a resource to use over the years for processing dreams and life.

Procedure

1. Work with one dream a week using the *Jungian-Senoi Dreamwork Manual* and other good books or processes on dreams. Share the results with someone who might also be working with dreams. You might even join a dream group for a few months and see what comes of it. Take the dreamwork manual and with a friend as your "dream partner" meet once a week and work with a method a week on your own dreams. This way you will develop a close relatedness and support for conscious growth and transformation, and you will also learn a complete dreamwork methodology which may add much to your life journey.

2. Look for themes and principles in your dreams which may have been evoked by working with this book.

Practice 20

PROCESSING CHILDHOOD DYNAMICS

"We return to inner childhood to redeem it and move forward in life."

Yes, back there in the past resides the little girl, the little boy which was us. The child archetype still lives within, redeemed or unredeemed.

To redeem one's childhood is to process the past to essence, to deal with the traumas and lost potentials there, to come to terms with how we did develop, to learn the nature of our own defense system so that we may become freed of it in adult life. The wondrous and the wounded child both live within now.

Many of us feel we have had either a happy childhood or one full of suffering, and if it was so painful only a fool would return to it. Right? Fools do many things necessary to the journey.

We return to inner childhood to redeem it and move forward in life. We return to childhood to graduate from childhood into adult life. For in truth most of us are still living as children in an adult world. We are living our parents' attitudes and expectations and not our own values and destiny, living an unfulfilled and compulsive life based on the needy child. We seek refuge in each other. We try to form the perfect relationship. We try to live out the family archetype in everything we do, hoping that at last someone will truly nurture and protect us in a way which never happened in childhood.

We remain unconsciously addicted to childhood.

We can live and die caught in the family archetype and never individuate ourselves. Calling our parents Mom and Dad even after we are grown-up adults in our own right. Living close to parents we may have little in common with. Trying to get our friends and lovers to nurture and respect us like our parents did or did not.

To be caught in the family archetype means relating to bosses, teachers, colleagues, parental figures, and other "authorities" as our parents. We try to create the dependency role all over again, hoping this time to have the perfect parents. They never materialize. The first and often great fall from grace is when our substitute parent does something which we feel is unfair, which does not seem to take our "rights" and aspirations into consideration. We sought their approval. We tried to be nice, to be good children, and we got stabbed in the back just like in childhood. It does not work to continue to play the parent-child dependency game as adults. To become an adult is to seek only relationships in which some measure of equality can exist. Even if you are less experienced than your supervisor, you can act as if you are contributing equally from your own level of awareness.

I am my childhood but I can move on in life.

Transforming childhood can mean redeeming the grace that was lost, healing the wounded child and actualizing the wondrous child. It can mean becoming truly parents to ourselves without being caught in the parental manipulations of others, including our own parents.

To help in this process I am writing a wonderful book called *Transforming Childhood*, available in a private reading edition direct from Journey Press. Its lessons can be used for individual and group work.

The Divine Child is one of the major symbols of the Central Archetype of the Self. Many religions have festivals devoted to the birth of the Divine Child. This is ageless wisdom that at the core of life is the Child, ever new, ever ready to seek fulfillment, ever ready to inherit the earth of our inner being.

Example

The event is an evening session of a weekend workshop on transforming childhood using the book *Transforming Childhood*. Each of us is to do a five minute enactment of a scene from childhood and we can ask others to act out different roles with us.

A woman in her middle thirties who has been going through a major transformation in the past two years chooses a typical scene from her childhood which also showed up recently in one of her dreams.

She is a girl of ten shopping with her mother. She finds a pretty dress for herself and shows it to her mother. Mother says, "It's a pretty dress, but wouldn't you like this one better?," or "We can make a more beautiful one at home, dear." Never once was this woman able to have her way with her mother.

In adult life she acted the helpless victim she had become. Then she struggled courageously with a serious illness and suffered it through, dealing with its psychological components as well as using holistic health treatment methods.

Now she was to reenact her childhood scene a second time, but to act differently so the situation, and its underlying pattern, could resolve itself. She sees the dress she wants, is denied by the mother, but this time forcefully takes her mother's wallet and says, "I'm buying this dress!"

Drama in the healing arena. What joy and vitality she showed here and in other places throughout the weekend. We can change. We can grow. The past does not have to chain us to our old ways. New life is always possible by processing our childhood experiences. The child is the healer of us all.

Procedure

1. As part of your journey keep making conscious the unconscious patterns and attitudes created in childhood which may be distorting your adult life. You can do dialogues and ask questions of yourself like the following.

   * Where is the child in me right now?
   * Where is my parent in me right now?
   * How am I seeking and encountering my parents out there in projections onto other people?
   * How am I demanding with others, acting out the child and projecting the parents onto them? Is it a projection of nurturing, of rejecting, of strength, of catastrophe?
   * What symbols of the child can I use to evoke renewal and new life for myself and others? The divine child? The laughing, playing child? Even the wounded and crying child to embody my sadness?
   * How creatively have I played with life today?

2. Attend workshops on the subject, work with a good therapist, work with the *Transforming Childhood* manual and other good books such as Francis Wicks's *The Inner World of Childhood.*

The Wondrous Child

The author at age three before his fall from grace.

All I wanted was a wonderful childhood...

The inner child is that part of of ourselves which is the source of spontaneity and new growth. If it gets maimed in childhood we become inhibited and too serious as adults.

Come on! Let go!

Practice 21

PERSONAL HEALING THROUGH THERAPY

"Therapy is being helped to help oneself."

Working in small and healing rooms on quiet streets in many cities are the therapists of the world. And to their doors come the searching and the troubled in life. The work is often in such secrecy that none hear about it, not the public certainly, and not even close friends and family.

Therapy is a modern name for a common practice which goes back thousands of years. Was there ever a time when someone did not go to someone else for support in working through life's issues? We can talk to our parents, grandparents, even our children or other relatives. But we find here that mostly they have strong biases about how we should be living our lives. It is as if the family or clan reputation is at stake in every major choice we make. So what if I am an alcoholic or my marriage dissolves? What does that have to do with you? And so on as we differentiate from our families.

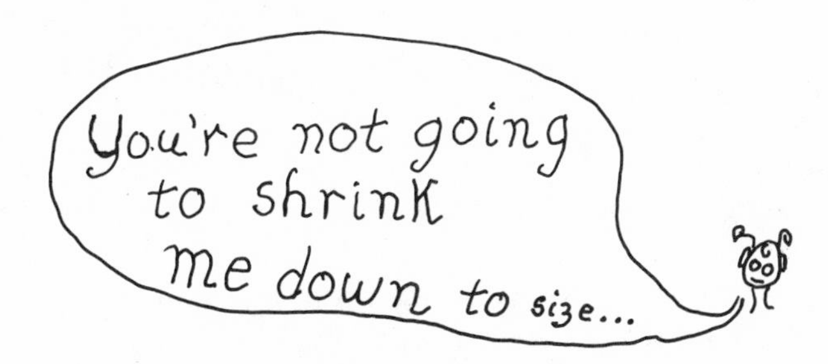

We could and do talk to our friends. For many of us a friend is someone we can talk to. Good friends listen and say things to make us feel good. Good friends do not challenge or get angry with us. We would leave them if they did.

Except in intimate relationships, of course. This is where many people seek and do therapy on each other.

Try not to use your intimate relationship for therapy, especially when you are dealing with intense problems.

If I dump my problems onto you and you dump your problems onto me, we are likely to make a mess of it. Neither one of us is that skilled in helping someone else solve problems

Yet, on the other hand most intimate relationships can be therapeutic, especially if they are balanced relationships. We learn by encountering each other. But the more we handle our own problems ourselves the better we feel and the better the relationship goes.

That which most distinguishes a professional therapist from an amateur one is that the professional helps the other person solve his or her own problems while the amateur tries to offer solutions and advice to the other person on how to deal with an issue.

Some professionally trained and licensed therapists do try to interpret and run their clients' lives. Avoid these therapists, psychologists, psychiatrists, like you would any coercive person in life.

Therapy is the art of opening a person up to his or her own healing.

An effective therapist is an objective one, a person with the ability to articulate the issues clearly, who teaches her clients how to do the same. A real therapist is a student of reality.

A good therapist is supportive and does not judge the person or his actions. Instead, she helps him replace judgment with feeling, clarification, and choice-making. Nothing is absolutely wrong in itself. There are only choices and their consequences. If I hurt my child, if I drink alcohol everyday, if I smoke compulsively, if I cannot hold onto some of the money I earn, then I have a problem and need help.

I do not need your judgment nor your punishment. I need your ability to help me get clearer on myself and on what I can do to change my behavior. I need to experience firsthand the emotional blocks which are evoking my destructive behavior.

Therapy is not always done with a professional therapist, in a one hour weekly session for several months. We might join a group of people like ourselves and benefit from how they are dealing with similar problems. We might go to special workshops on topics such as being more loving or expressing anger safely. And then again we can do therapy with ourselves by keeping a journal and working with a book such as this.

Therapy is most called for when we feel nearly overwhelmed by a life or personality problem. Better to seek help in dealing with a relationship crisis than to go it alone and have the ground fall out from under you. Better to establish a therapeutic relationship with a skilled professional than succumb to debilitating depression which wipes out your creative energy.

Therapy is just as needed at times for the normal and creatively functioning person as for those suffering severe mental illness. The wise person becomes strong in life not by simply going it alone but by seeking competent help whenever necessary.

A Destructive Therapist

A friend of mine, herself a good therapist, recently went looking for a therapist for herself. She had to have sessions with five before she found the right one. Along the way she had two sessions with Dr. D., who was well respected by his colleagues. She shared some of her issues and when he repeatedly interrupted her with interpretations of her behavior she challenged him and said she did not feel he was really helping her relate better in her life, since he himself was such a bad example. He refused to acknowledge her point and she left upset, but she decided to return for another session, just in case she was projecting negativity on him.

Their second session fared no better. He still persisted in telling her what she was like, provoking a still stronger confrontation from her in which she said she would not allow herself to be treated in this way and was not coming back. Dr. D. countered this time with the interpretation that she was just running away from someone who refused to let her manipulate him. It was again her fault. She could not have her feelings respected there. No transformation could occur.

An Open Therapist

Several years ago when I was attempting to develop a viewpoint of my own after nine years of analysis with a therapist, she suggested I see a colleague of hers. My first and subsequent meetings with him were a breath of fresh air. He listened intently to what I had to say but did not put forth his own opinion. Instead, he asked question after question. "Now why do you feel that? And what is behind that?" With his simple and direct questioning he freed me to be myself. He had no answers for me but he knew how to help me directly find my own truth. I felt freed of outside judgments, and from then on I changed my life radically and never looked back.

In my own work as a therapist I also try to maintain objectivity by bringing up both sides of an issue and asking questions which help a person to explore who they are in relation to the issues they face, and what they can do.

The Practice

1. Evaluate your present relationships. Are you using some of them for personal therapy in dealing with life's problems? Are you really being helped? Are you changing? Is the friendship honest and real, or is it one-sided and based on expectations? Who does more of the talking?

2. What life problems are you having today and how are you dealing or not dealing with them? Which ones do you need help with and why?

3. What do you mean you cannot afford therapy? There are good therapists in low cost clinics. If you budget your money you will see where you can cut back on other things for a few months. There is nothing wrong with taking a small part-time job to create the extra money for therapy. What are your priorities in life? What is more important than spending money on your own health and growth?

4. What attitudes might be blocking you from seeking therapeutic help for your problems? Where do these attitudes come from? What are the fears behind them?

5. Give your reactions to this affirmation as you try it out for yourself. **I am more and more able to seek good support for myself in whatever I do.**

6. If you still feel you do not need therapy now, and you may not, then why not? Are you making creative changes in your life? Are you changing in response to others? Are you actively transforming blocks and outworn attitudes? Good, if so, then you are on your way.

Ten Essential Points About Choosing a Therapist

1. Go into therapy when you are feeling overwhelmed in any of the major areas of life, such as relationships, work, personal emotions, direction and purpose in life.

2. In finding a therapist, ask people you know and trust for referrals. Personal recommendations by others who have experienced the therapy is worth far more than degrees and licenses.

3. Because a person has a degree or license or is a religious leader does not qualify them as a good therapist. Having a license and an advanced degree in counseling or psychology at the M.A., M.D. or Ph.D. level only shows that a person has had a basic training in therapeutic interaction. It does not show that they have gone through personal transformation in their own lives or that they have talent for doing therapy.

4. What makes a good therapist is the ability to help effect healing in another. This can only happen if a therapist has developed an open, expressive personality and has gone through personal transformation. Ask about their own therapy or how they have helped others.

5. A good therapist is also one who has trained extensively in the field and who continues training and is in association with other therapists. Ask about the background of your prospective therapist.

6. There are a number of good people who can help you in your healing process who are not licensed or have not had university training. They may call themselves ministers, priests, nurses, psychic counselors, teachers or whatever. Ask about where they received their experience and find out what they believe makes them qualified to do therapy or counseling with you.

7. Relationship counseling is quite different from individual or group therapy. For relationship problems go only to someone skilled in training you in communications, issue-solving, and open, honest emotional interaction at the feeling level. Ask if you will be trained in communication skills so that you can solve your own issues together.

8. Talking therapy of whatever school is good for bringing out issues and developing new perspectives on yourself and life. It helps you see yourself and your own issues in new ways so that you may know yourself better as you deal with life. If your prospective therapist gives you advice or evaluates your behavior as good and bad, find another therapist. You have found a substitute parent and not someone who can be objective in letting you make your own choices. If the talk between you seems too rational and conceptual then your therapist is not helping you get to a feeling and emotional level about yourself. Ask why this is not happening for you and what you can both do about it.

9. Some therapy is primarily emotional rather than talk and thought oriented. If you are too verbal and distance yourself from reality with ideas, seek non-verbal therapies, such as Reichian bodywork, Gestalt, Jungian-Senoi dreamwork, Psychodrama, etc. These are powerful therapies which should only be done with skilled practitioners you can trust. If your first session does not feel right, try someone else. You do not have to have a reason not to go back to this therapist.

10. You will resist therapy. All of us have negative reactions from time to time. We don't want to go to our session, or we feel the therapist is an awful person. All resistance is really resisting a part of ourselves. Express your negativity freely in your session, but go. If you and your therapist can process the negativity, you will feel yourself changing. If not, go to someone else. You are choosing change. Change involves dealing with the negative, as well as the positive. Ask your therapist to help you deal with your own negativity about therapy and about him.

Practice 22

JOURNALWORK

"Reflection on life is what gives
Life to life."

We each have a book of our life. It may be one we write, it may be one we only talk, as with all the stories about our own experiences we tell our friends. This book may also be received in a dream.

What does it mean to have a book of one's own life? Many of us may not feel gifted in literary writing, but that is not necessary to keep a journal. If you write letters to friends and family, you are in effect keeping a journal, a journal which you give away to others unless you keep copies of all your letters.

We write to know ourselves. What we share with others is really what we learn about ourselves.

A journal is a bound blank book in which we write our thoughts and feelings about certain experiences in our day. Or we might simply express feelings, writing big and boldly, getting the energy out. We can add or draw images to better symbolize our significant experiences. We can have dialogues, or conversations with inner figures, to help resolve certain issues. We can write down some of our more major dreams and work with them.

A journal is not a diary. A diary is usually described as a bound book in which the entries are factual descriptions, dated, for later recall.

In a journal it is helpful to date your entries, but they need not be factual. Instead, what you write can be feeling and imaginative. You are speaking with your own soul, not the exact tongue of the historians. You can include things which might make sense to no one else but you. You will often write only or mainly about inner events instead of outer events you would include in a diary. You will even write what you might consider garbage into your journal as you write to get your feelings out.

You're not going to catch me on paper!

Why would I choose to keep a personal journal?

Why live life itself if you have little or no purpose for it? Life is hard work much of the time, hardly worth the effort if all you are doing is trying to keep your life going. Life is more than the living of life. It is for living the purpose of life. But what if you have not yet found your purpose?

To find your purpose you must know yourself, reflect upon who you are and what your life is all about. **Reflection on life is what gives Life to life.** And regular journalwork is one useful method for reflecting upon and processing your life. We must take the time to go inner to go outer. To simply fixate on everyday life itself is to be caught in it, living it on its terms, dominated by it and rendered unconscious by the whole surge of life itself.

C.G. Jung has formulated a wonderful term discovered from the medieval alchemists. *Contra naturum*—to go against nature for the sake of increasing one's consciousness. It is only by opposing nature that we can establish enough distance to observe her closely. If I am totally caught up in expressing my sexuality I will have a hard time dealing with it choicefully and integrating it into the rest of my life.

Journals are private affairs. **It is a great indiscretion to read someone else's journal without their permission. Do not take on what you are not ready to deal with.** Reading someone else's letters or journals is always an invasion of privacy. The journal writer wants a private place in which to process his or her stuff by being able to express freely without fear or repercussions. And for the intruder into privacy a burden is created in that you have taken into your psyche some emotional information which you may well have trouble dealing with.

Much can be done by communing with oneself in a private and real book of one's own, our personal journal. We need to process by getting things out of our hearts and onto paper, both the positive and negative. **And the more we reveal ourselves, the more we accept ourselves.**

I and my life are worth writing about so that I may be more creative, imaginative and conscious with my life.

The Procedure

1. Try keeping a journal for three months. Buy a nicely bound blank book and begin. Date your entries and even give titles to them. Record your dreams and any experiences which have energy, positive or negative, for you. Keep writing in a feeling way until what you have written about seems complete or resolved. If you decide to include dreamwork, write your dream on the left hand page and your comments and dreamwork on the right hand page. Let people close to you know your journal is private and not to be read. Do not leave it out in the open as a symbolic invitation to be looked into. The devil is the temptation of the righteous.

2. Create a journal of your work with this book, or another book of special significance to you. This might include rewriting quotes from the book, writing out the exercises, or simply making comments about how various things strike you. You might also include life examples from your own life illustrating the points. In other words, you could use working with this book to process and realize the significance of your own life experience.

3. You might decorate your journal cover with paint, pictures,symbols, etc. This is truly your own book. Why be confined to reading everybody else's books about life? Make one of your own about your own life. Take time, especially before bed, to write about what is significant to you right now. Write when the energy is high and also when it needs to be evoked.

Practice 23

DIALOGUE

"Dialogue is relatedness revealed."

Dialogue is an age-old method of revealing information about oneself from oneself. The known part of us, the ego, actively engages an unknown part of ourselves and through the encounter builds the relationship and receives important information about oneself and about life.

All too often we ask others for wisdom and advice about a life situation or problem when we could make better use of the energy by dialoging directly with the problem itself.

If I am angry with someone I interact with, should I express my anger to that person directly, or would it be better to handle my anger myself and wait until I have dealt with my own anger before approaching the other person I have an issue with?

I am my own anger. It does not belong to another. I can deal with it. **I am angry, ultimately, only with myself.**

Dialogue then with the image of your outer adversary as an inner adversary. First we explore the issues we are angry about. Then we call into our consciousness an image and feeling for the person we dislike. Then, writing quickly, we vent feelings and ask our adversary questions and write whatever comes into our heads as response. We do not censor what we hear. We simply respond to it and listen and write.

This dialogue with an inner person or another part of ourselves often gets into a flow in which it comes almost automatically until the energy resolves itself and we have our new unity or a resolution to the conflict.

For example, using dialogue in dealing with anger I might ask my adversary,

* What are you doing to make me angry?
* What can I do to feel better about you?
* How can I stop you from making me angry?
* What can I do to change?

The spiritual effect of dealing with anger as an inner problem can well lead to a healing change in the relationship even before you both talk together. This is because people who evoke our anger get our shadow projections. Once you remove or alter a shadow projection through dialogue and integration the whole relationship changes.

Within each of us are the archetypes, the energy-creating dynamics of the psyche. Often these essences are out of relation with each other and with the ego. Wholeness is only a potential and the person, like a victim riddled full of holes, is prey to a host of conflicting archetypes. Integration means dealing with the conflicts by making choices and creating experiences of new relatedness among all those dynamics of the psyche. **Dialogue is relatedness revealed.**

The ego can keep dialoguing over several months and record in a journal these spiritual conversations with many different parts of oneself. One can dialogue with,

* One's ego. Ask it what it needs to let go of.
* One's shadow. Ask it to come forward and express itself.
* One's persona. Ask it to be less fearful.
* One's dream source. Ask it for a dream or how to better remember dreams.
* One's anger. Ask it to tell you what is making you angry.

Dialogue can be used almost daily in our ongoing relation with our inner self, not higher self. Never dialogue with the higher self only, since that easily leads to spiritual inflation, or being puffed up by the good and the light, sinless side of life. God is not interested in how good you are but in how whole you can become.

If you dialogue only with your higher self, what happens with your lower self, your shadow, your sex, your anima, your animus, etc.? Better by far in terms of wholeness to gradually have dialogues with many sides of yourself.

Dialogue is also a major dreamwork method of the Jungian-Senoi approach. Using this method the dreamer writes up key issues and questions about the dream, picks the dream character with the greatest energy, positive or negative, and then asks it to respond to the questions.

To summarize in a general principle, **Inner dialogue helps establish relatedness and integration with the various parts of oneself.**

Example

Several years ago when I was a beginning therapist in a residential treatment center for highly disturbed teenagers I had a conversation with my director which helped change my life.

Another psychotherapist, younger than I, was somehow always getting on my nerves. He would subtly oppose me in staff meetings and make remarks which would just inflame me. I brought this up with my director, an extremely intuitive and gifted woman.

She said, "You know he is evoking you on purpose. He loves to get you angry."

This shocked me. I had not realized that it was deliberate. I wanted my director to do something about it, but instead she put the responsibility back on my shoulders. I was the one who would have to go through a personal transformation since I was the one being upset.

"All right," I eventually conceded, "what can I do about it?"

"Do what I do," was her reply. "When I am upset with someone or someone is upset with me I have an inner dialogue with the spirit of that person and ask them what is going on or what I can do to effect reconciliation. Even if it takes years I always try to effect reconciliation with others. Almost always as you listen to that person's spirit with your inner ear you will receive information about your own shadow and the need to integrate it."

I followed her teaching, relieved that there might be a way to transform the situation without somehow making him leave me alone, which I apparently did not have the direct power to do. The results were everything I could hope for. My inner voice represented by him said that he was being competitive with me because he wanted to better himself, and he used me as an example. The inner voice also said that he most got to me when I was feeling arrogant and therefore vulnerable. It said that it did not matter if he opposed me because he only had power over me when he evoked my shadow, and if I integrated my shadow and could see my own arrogance and competitiveness as a man, he would never be able to upset me as much again. This worked and worked beautifully. He still tried to get my goat from time to time but I recognized that since I was the older man he needed to compete with me, and that I always had the power and competence to hold my own. The recognition that I did at times act arrogantly when I wanted to act with authority opened me to welcoming his "help" in pointing out my shadow to me. As a result my effectiveness increased and I was seldom threatened by his behavior. We never became friends and we had further confrontations. But from then on, because of my dialoging, I could hold my own and not feel undermined by anything he would try to do. I believe I earned his respect, and I embodied more of my shadow also. For he was arrogant too, and I had been unconsciously sitting in judgment on him.

Transformation had come for us through dialogue with my shadow and a choice for wholeness instead of superiority. The general principle might be, **To deal with your shadow, accept and create with its energy.**

The Procedure

1. First dialogue with your dialogue censor. Ask it any of the following questions,

* What are you like?
* How would you try to keep the flow from happening in my dialogues?
* What can I do to get you to help me with my dialogues?
* I want you to stay out of my dialogue, so have your say right now, say anything you want, then leave my dialogue alone.

2. In dialoguing with some figure, a person or dream being,

* Make a list of key questions such as, why are you doing what you are doing to me? Or, why are you in my dream, or in my life, right now? Or, what do you want from me? Or, what can I do to be effective with you?
* Write down anything which comes into your head without censoring. Give your own responses also, "I like that," "I don't agree with you," etc.
* Dialogue until you feel blocked or feel a sense of resolution. Then live what you have learned.

I am more and more willing to talk with parts of myself to aid my own wholeness.

Practice 24

BEING FULLY IN THE MOMENT

"Everything happens now, not later."

This will be short and sweet. We are dealing with essence here. The most outrageous thing we can say is that all of us only give part of ourselves to each moment and spread the rest of ourselves out into that which does not exist, namely, the past and the future. We shrink from being fully present in the now by either going backward into memories or forward into fantasies. There may be appropriate times to really pursue a memory or a fantasy to arrive at the essence of the experience, but so often we use memory and fantasy as defensive escapes from everyday reality. Cut it out and live in the moment. The moment is all you or any of us have. These are the principles and their practices.

* **Whatever exists is real and this is what we deal with. Everything happens now, not later.**

Much of the time we want things to be different than they are. We resist reality, or things as they are. We cause pain by resisting what is. We try to impose our wants and desires onto an unyielding universe. We may even seem to get what we want, but often we do not want what we get.

We learn to make our desires and intentions consistent with what is possible in reality. We do not waste even a second on what cannot be actualized. We fall in love and the other person does not love us? Immediately, if I have become a realist, I yield to reality and take my love experience as relevant only to me and not to the other person. Learn to play the game of love well. Learn not to pursue love relationships with those who do not love you. Do not try to change anyone either. You only have power to change yourself and not the other person.

* **I deal with that which exists, not with what could exist. I prepare for the Now, not the Later. The future is created out of what I do now, not what I do later.**

Too often we become upset by things which do not exist. We are in a relationship and are afraid our lover will leave us. But ground yourself. Has your lover left you, or are you in fact not feeling close to each other right now? Future fears must be seen as present realities. If you are not close to each other now, that is what you deal with. That grounds the situation in the now. If you want to keep the relationship going a long time, you can worry and strategize all you want about the future. But what about the present moment? The relationship will stay together or not stay together based on how both of you handle each moment together. That is where you put your efforts. Not on what might happen some day farther on.

Too much anxiety gets bound up in endless speculation about what could go wrong in life. Often we hear the accusation, "but what if such and such had happened?" Well, only one thing happened and that is what we deal with. Cut the speculation and get with the now, the reality immediately before you.

* **I spend my energy and time only where I have the chance to be effective. Where I have no power to change things I let the issue go.**

Effectiveness is the ability to change reality in a given direction. To be effective I need power and consciousness of what exists.

Can you change your parents? Can you change your boss? Can you change your lover? Can you change your child? Can you change yourself? Can you change your adversary?

We learn to wait until the moment is right and then make a decisive choice which may change the situation. Where you have power use it in the service of reality and your values. Where you have not the power to change something, accept reality as it is and do not spend time or energy there where you cannot be effective. Realistically, you only have time and energy for those things you can be effective in. So use what you have well.

* **I have everything I need right now in this and every moment to deal with and actualize the full potential of the situation.**

Part of our sense of feeling overwhelmed in problem situations is that we do not recognize that we have everything we need to handle each and every situation which arises in life. We become caught and anxious and immediately we let ourselves feel inadequate. We think we need to be rescued. We act helpless so someone will become a parent to us and come and bail us out. The results are often poor, to say the least. We have failed our own potential. One of the great life tasks is to become more and more adequate to dealing effectively with reality.

Actualizing the full potential in a situation might mean we ask for help, but we do not act helpless. That we are not, because we are using the principle of fully actualizing the moment. First we accept reality, then we actualize it, we develop the full potentials for growth and meaning from the givens available.

* **Do everything now, not later. Do only what is essential in life and let the rest go.**

Each moment of my life I can ask myself what is the most essential thing needing doing now? What is most possible in this situation? What I come up with is an approach which is not essentially reactive. I do not go around just trying to keep up with the difficulties of life in a sort of survivalist doctrine. I anticipate the moment. I am ready for its eventualities, and I enter fully into the now, taking what comes my way and living it to its fullest extent. I do not waste time and energy on what is non-essential to my life, on that which blocks the full appreciation of the the moment.

* **We choose life in order for it to choose us.**

"What are my choices?" Not, "What are my endless possibilities?" Choices ground us in the moment. Choices limit us to the Now. Endless possibilities diffuse us, spread us out into fantasy land where nothing really happens which makes a difference to the quality of life lived in the real world. If you have fantasies, actualize them or let them go. Do not daydream on forever over a sea of nothingness. If you want to get going with your life, actualize the moment, every moment, and to do this you need to be making choices. Ask not, "What would I like?" but "What is possible?" What are my options for choice? That is what I deal with and I let the rest go, go to the winds forever.

The Practice

1. Work with the above principles and make them your own.Do you now commit yourself to living in present reality as much as you possibly can? Are you willing to let go of whatever might stand in the way of this commitment? If so, do so now. Work with each of the principles and write out or talk about ways you will actualize them. Nothing else matters.

2. List some of the things you do when you find yourself not completely in the moment. Out of this develop some intentions for living more fully in the moment. What are your most difficult times? Your easiest times?

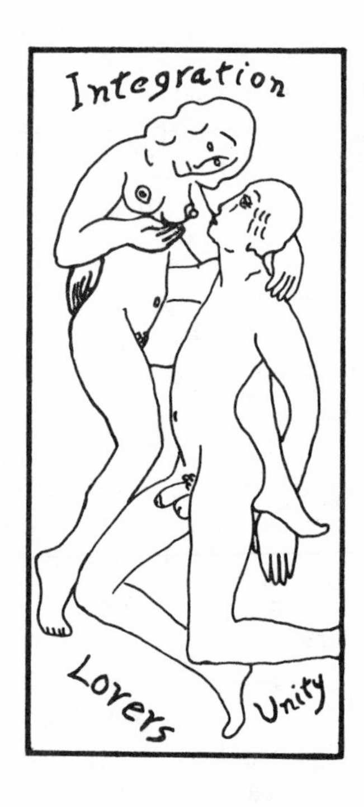

Practice 25

FINDING A SPIRITUAL PERSPECTIVE

"To become spiritual is to live life without identifying with it."

Consider these questions.

* How am I dealing with this world?
* What is the style with which I am living life?
* Are any of us really all that conscious of what we are doing with our lives?

Consciousness is the key to action. Without consciousness, we will act. That is for sure. But we will not know why we act or to what purpose.

You think you know why you are doing what you are doing? You feel that you are really achieving what you want to be achieving?

Usually we do what we identify with, and what we identify with we are largely unconscious about.

I am a jogger but why do I run? Will this help fulfill my life's purpose?

I am a mother but why do I nurture? Am I really expressing my core personality or responding automatically to others' needs?

I am an engineer but am I using my energy for my own life or is it all going for the company?

We identify with what we do and that makes us unconscious. And what we are unconscious of we can hardly change.

Simply, most of us are spending a good eighty to ninety percent of our lives upholding the fabric of civilization and spending little time on our real selves. The culture demands of us our daily work and rewards us with praise, promotion and prosperity. The system runs our lives and we have little creativity left to reflect on our individuality and the meaning of life.

This is what is meant when it is said that we live in a secular world. When we are identified with what we do we will be little able to change ourselves and explore meaning.

We are too busy changing our children, changing our company, changing the calendar, changing the world, to have much energy to really change ourselves.

What if we spent a good fifty percent of our waking day in self-directed and meaning-oriented growth activity? What then?

Civilization might fall apart? The machines would go into disrepair? Technological innovation would come to a halt? The arts would lose freshness? Politics would lose its fervor?

Not so! World culture would take another leap forward. To be one-sided is always to work against oneself. If we spent half the time in self-reflective and inward activities, our outer activities would be less in number but far greater in value and focus. **Too much compulsive outer activity creates a scattered and exhausting life.** Where is the purpose and meaning in putting so much time into carrying the Goliath of civilization forward, or closer to its own abyss?

The Spiritual Quest

We have always known it. We have felt it deep within our own hearts. We have even been open to it in times of stress and life transitions. It has been as a gleam, a light seen through a door down a long hallway.

But how many of us have seen this possibility of light and followed it to its source, forsaking in the process complete identification with the outer world?

To be spiritual is to seek to make all one's choices within a context of conscious wholeness and meaning.

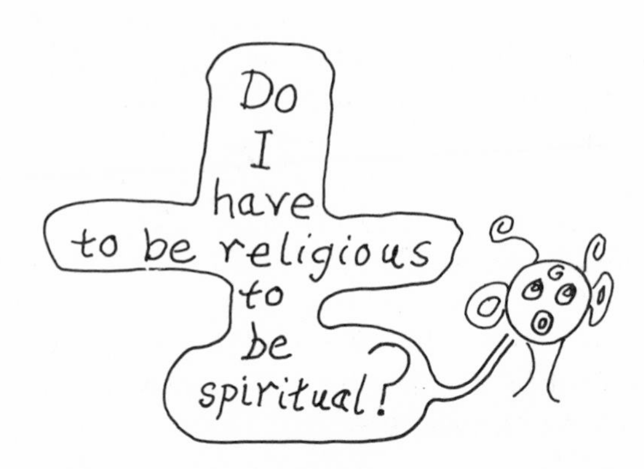

To be spiritual is to seek the meaning at the core, not the surface, of things.

To become spiritual is to choose to do only those things which contribute meaning and healing to one's life.

To live spiritually is to live the transformational life in each moment. And what is the transformational life?

* A life lived seeking to create the deepest value in every situation.
* A life based on letting go of old ways and actualizing new potentials for wholeness.
* A life created out of following a source greater than ego.
* A life freed from identification with the world and its values.
* A life fully productive in the world, yet not of the world but of the heart, of the inner core and soul of one's being.
* A life lived focused on experiences of transcendence grounded in the here and now.

We can change through seeking spiritual growth because being spiritual means living the spirit of the thing, the essence of the event, the core of each being. We will change and change for the better into a more meaningful and creative life because we are yielding ourselves to source energies. We are daily choosing the most resolving experiences available in life.

* Such as embracing and living the energy of the enemy as well as the friend.
* Such as giving up outworn ways of acting and perceiving.
* Such as reflecting upon and making conscious whatever we do and whatever happens to us.

Whatever happens is real and what is real has something to teach us about life.

One person experiences physical symptoms, such as a back ache, and runs off to the doctor to receive treatment instead of also using the painful symptom to explore ways of changing habits causing the pain.

Another represses a feeling of tension and grabs for a cigarette, some alcohol, TV or senseless reading.

A person working spiritually convinces no one of anything directly, as in preaching or a sales talk. Such a person influences people through understanding and being connected to the sources of a meaningful life.

The person committed to realizing the meaning of one's life is a person,

* Who is actively working with making conscious one's life through therapeutic and spiritual acts such as dreamwork, bodywork, therapy, meditation, journalwork, etc.
* Who follows inner guidance as much as or more than outer guides, who follows intuitions and feelings, who uses dreams as a source for new perspective, who uses feedback from others to become aware of one's own self-evaluations and feelings.
* Who is often or continuously developing and making stronger a center within oneself. This is a center embodying the integrative-transformative functions of the Self, which more and more encompasses the opposites within and without.
* Who develops meaningful relationships based on mutual honesty, common sharing, and a commitment to process whatever gets evoked in the relationship so that the experience together may be full of resolutions and new life.
* Whose central devotion is to actualizing source energies.

A person journeying meaningfully through life is one who focuses on,

* Creating new consciousness of who one is and what is actual in reality.
* Living not just at the surface of things but at the core, following life principles which are both meaningful and realistic.

To serve the Self, the Central Archetype of wholeness, differentiation and integration, is at once the goal and the process. What we are most devoted to we live daily as well as ultimately. **What lives, lives now.** There is no tomorrow. What happens happens today, and now is the avenue of the possible.

We move forward taking only the essence of the past with us if we are working consciously. **And what is our goal, what is the open door, our vision of the future? To passionately want and live life to the full, actualizing the most meaningful potentials available and constantly enlarging the range of what we will deal with by going through and beyond the next fear.**

A Person On The Way

A person whose most major life goal is the realization of a meaningful destiny might exhibit the following characteristics,

* Devotion to personal growth as much as to occupational or family work.

* Living a balanced life whenever possible, combining outer activities with inner activities. The feeling, emotional life is balanced with the working life. Having experiences of being alone with oneself in meditation, journalwork, hiking, etc., is balanced with being with others, working and sharing together.

* That within whatever level of income and use of time one has, one is always creating a "portion of freedom" used for developing new potentials. Never spend all your money or time on what you are already doing.

A person on The Way is one who,

* Daily develops the art of choice-making, thus increasing the range, meaning and effectiveness of one's choices. One does not drift through life simply reacting to everything, but actively seeks the most valuable potential in each situation and actualizes it.

* Deals daily with the regressive pull, that force which can make us sleepy, lazy and ineffective, usually based on the ego's fear of the future and its habit of seeking only pleasure in life. Dealing with the regressive pull means enduring the pain and discomfort necessary to living solidly in reality and realizing the individualized life.

* Deals often with evil and destructiveness, not by moralistically avoiding and repressing our own potentials for destruction and imperfection, but by embracing evil. Yes, encompassing the destructive force in life without identifying with it, and by owning it within oneself. Repression and avoidance create greater destructiveness. Encompassing, making conscious and transforming any energy leads to new life.

What awaits us in the process, the wound and priceless jewel in the rainbow, is life, life lived to the core of our being, life which encompasses the opposites, life based on resolution and healing, life, an open door to death and to the center.

We have a soul, each one of us, at once simple and profound, ephemeral and necessary. The experience is what we live. The essence is what we create and let go of.

Like a sun shimmering on the waters, like a moon reflected in a mountain lake, like the touch of a breeze on a hillside, like a clear spring flowing in a forest, like a human kiss never forgotten, like a dark well, empty but full, the soul is there, still, ungraspable, image and essence.

Will we be ready? Are we ready now?

The Choice, The Work, the Journey begins today and each day of our lives. You are invited into the open room, the subtle path, and what will you find?

Mystery, ordinariness, the human element, jewels and dung, laughter and cunning, tears, anger and relief, a most important conversation, a purchase made, a marriage feast, a vast disappointment, an old shoe.

Who knows the future, yet we travel into it? Who knows the past, yet we are held back by it?

We have then and always that one pure choice, the action taken now, the Yes with no serious regrets, the step forward.

The choice is made. Everything the same? The veil lifted at last?

Who knows what is about to be born in me if I will let it be born through choice?

Practice 26

TRANSFORMING YOUR DYING

"Life is the goal of life, and dying the process."

Death as the Way to Life

Death is a fearful word to all of us. Not only do we have the physical death of ourselves or others we know, but we have also the many deaths which occur in life. The death of relationship, of a job, of an experience, of a former life stage, as when we graduate from high school. We are glad to get out of there, just as we are happy to get away from our parents, but still. Still we hate to leave all of the past behind as we move forward into the future. The young are eager for the future while the old are reminiscent about the past. **There is no past where the future is not born.**

We can approach the experience of dying and death with a set of principles and practices which help us encompass this reality. For death, as well as life, is a reality. We die with the living and are born with the dead.

In one very real sense, we do not fear death, we fear dying. Once dead we have lost awareness of the life state and so do not experience the total loss of ourselves. But dying is different. There we are aware that our life is ending and we often try to resist this fact, causing pain and perhaps transformation. Dying is the rub, is that which hurts the body and frees the soul. For is not life more than body and soul more than life?

Is life the living of life, or is the goal of life the approach to death and the culmination of life? Is life for the living of life or is there something more? Respond to these questions yourself. Indeed we each answer them with our own lives.

Many of us hope against hope that something of our individual selves transcends the physical death. We would like to believe, as the ancient Egyptians did, that there is life after death, eternal life. True, their mummies survived thousands of years, as did their culture. This is the immortality they achieved, the immortality of dry flesh and carved stone. What is there for the rest of us who have not the resources of the ancients to preserve something of our essence for posterity? Everyone seeks some semblance of transcending their own physical deaths. For many it is the producing of children. Our children will live after us and themselves produce children. But my children are not me. They have their own lives to live, as I live mine. Others join some cause or religion and identify with it, hoping that they will achieve some transcendence through their cause or religion. Yes, the religions survive, at least for a time, and they have a body of beliefs to comfort their dying, such as reincarnation and heaven. They also have burial ceremonies, graveyards and lists of the departed.

What good is the survival of a name? Shakespeare's name survives through his works, but his life is gone. He writes no new plays nor loves anyone simply because his plays are enacted. The words survive but the human does not. And so what is transcendence? How can I tie into what is essential to life, yet transcends life? How can I encompass death in life? For surely death will encompass my life.

We could end now, just having raised the questions, having raised issues to which there are no answers, only responses. For who has come back from the dead to tell us whether there is more on the other side? Who is to say whether all thoughts of a life hereafter are not merely projections of life potentials unlived here?

If we go on with our exposition, we will have to content ourselves not with ultimate questions, those questions which tend to produce dogmas, but with process.

Okay, I am going to die and I fear it. I don't want to die yet. I'm not ready to go. I have so much to do yet.

What is it we most fear then? Perhaps the fear of death is actually the fear of dying before we have truly found life? Once we find life, once we find and commit ourselves to a process which helps us live life to the fullness of our destiny, then maybe we will be ready and even welcome death when the day arrives. Think of it! On a certain day in your own life, your head will be cut off, you will be executed by the grim reaper just as surely as I or anyone else will be. Are you ready today to go? If you are not ready for this ultimate in the journey, why haven't you prepared yourself? What do you think you have been given life for? To squander it, even passionately, on whatever you feel like doing or on what others want you to do?

What have we each been given life for? That is the question. Let death be our answer. Let death come when it may. We can be ready for it by practicing dying daily to life. That is our answer, our response to this ultimate experience of death. **Life is the goal of life, and dying the process.**

Principles

To live, die daily to life. We do not look back or dwell in memories of what was, no matter how beautiful or wonderful. The past is dead even though it may become a grave of unlived life. To live we sacrifice the old, we sacrifice anything which would keep us hanging on, old values, parental expectations, wonderful experiences, old friends and lovers, and the unlived life, the basis of all nostalgia.

We orient ourselves toward the future by living its potentials in the now. If your focus is on potentials you do not need the past. Potentials come in dreams, in destiny, in whatever comes our way to be dealt with and actualized.

Who has time for yesterday when tomorrow is on the way? But in order to be fully present to the moment and its potentials we have to die, we have to sacrifice the old for the new, we have to say No to all which would oppose the present moment. I know we got married, but what does that have to do with anything? If we do not have the potential for a fulfilling marriage now, why stay married? We may have to divorce, kill the old life, feel the loss and grief because in our divorce part of ourselves will die. But it is gone anyway. Let's live now. Ruthless? No, simply courageous and extremely realistic. **Fear not death in the future. The only death there is is what is past.**

We choose dying in order to live. We choose to let go of our bodies, our desires, our hopes, our fears, our unreality. Better to disidentify from your body now through bodywork and awareness rather than have cancer slowly take your body from you in disease.

We choose to live at the edge of risk. We go to the edge where death is because there also is life. We must be willing to lose all if we would gain all. We risk failure and diminishment in order to have increase. **We dwell in insecurity to become secure.** We encompass the opposites in order to achieve wholeness in each moment. Those who are afraid to die, who are afraid to give up the known for the unknown, will not live at the edge of risk, facing death in each moment.

I choose to live in all my dying. Immortality is living fully in the now. In the now there is no death, and once the now is gone there is only death. Death is when there is no Now. We sacrifice, let go of, everything which prevents us from being in the present moment. Fears, memories, hopes, strictures, unconscious or collective attitudes, false images, egocentricities. We use the death process, the killing process, to clear away the stuff which prevents us from being in the present moment. The paradox is that we use death to create life. Everything must go which stands in the way of the present moment. When something stressful happens let go to all its potentials in the moment. Do not dwell in memories and past dramas or attitudes of inadequacy. This is anxiety.

Do only the essential in life. We kill ourselves by wasting our time on projects and people which don't really enhance our own fulfillment and destiny. Answering the telephone all the time. Reading junk mail. Watching television regularly or reading books all the time instead of creating something of your own or getting out into the world and participating in it, camping, dancing, traveling, working.

Fight the regressive pull so that you do not give up on life. There are many things we do to ourselves which represent the death force instead of the life force. Not exercising or eating well. Over-working, smoking, drinking excessively, extraverting without having much creative time alone. Being too involved in others' lives. Worrying or giving time and energy to areas and issues which we have no power to change. Letting depression and loneliness take over instead of continually seeking the opportunities which are there for us in reality. These are examples of the living grave we dig for ourselves. You don't have to live life fully. It used to be called the Devil. Now we call it the regressive pull just waiting to carry us away.

Search for that which is at the core of all things. Perhaps as I align my life to following the direction of the Self, the center within and without, I will not only enhance my life but that of the Self also. By making it more realizable in myself I may be making it more realizable for others. That which transcends my individuality is the archetype of the Self. I give my life to the Self and it gives life to me and all those who seek it. My soul becomes part of the filament, the intangible glistening, meshed in with countless others to make the radiant whole, the encompassing center spiraling outward as it creates its inward journey through light and dark into the hand of the Unnameable, the All which transcends All, the spark that never fails, and I somehow can live and maybe die as part of all that.

Life is living consciously. Until we have committed ourselves to making ourselves and our lives conscious we are living but not alive to life. Life lives us. We do not live it. If we do not know who we are, who we are does not know us. Most people die not having known themselves or the nature of life and death. They have lived unconsciously and die unconsciously. They have continually sought unconsciousness when the pain or going gets rough. They have not been able to take life as it is and have drugged themselves with unconsciousness at every turn. Becoming conscious is the second birth. Staying conscious is the primary task.

The Death Experience

Once dead what do we know? No one has come back from the dead to tell us. Our body dies. Our ego dies. We no longer make choices or influence this life directly. We may contact people in dreams and visions, but to communicate rather than choose is quite different. Perhaps the presences in dreams and visions are the projections of inner content from the living? We simply do not know. Perhaps choice is taken away from us at death. Or is it?

The reality is that in all likelihood we do not survive physical death as individual beings. Our individuality, our choice-making, our living the earthly life of pleasure, pain and meaning, vanishes. Death is final. We have lived once in this body and that's it, past life memories to the contrary. Past life experiences seem to be inner experiences expressed outwards, not bodies in action in former times, unless where there is no past, present, and future everything is simultaneous. But in reality death is final, and we can accept its finality to really live now.

Those who would believe in reincarnation or life after death experiences can ask themselves, what purpose does it serve to think that I was someone else in a former life, or will be someone, or an ant, in a new lifetime? If your belief keeps you from living life fully because you believe you will have another chance, then look at that. If you are afraid to die, to face the physical death, then question your present beliefs about life after death, let go of them if you can and face death, the adversary. Does she wear the veils of reincarnation for you or is her abyss real?

The Dying Experience

Which is better? To die slowly of cancer, or to die suddenly in one's sleep of a heart attack? With one we can die consciously, knowing that we are dying. We can go through a transformative process which we may never have attempted before in our lives. Those who die without knowing they are dying have the disadvantage in that they do not have the chance to face the ultimate and to consciously resolve their lives. However, those who consciously practice a transformative process throughout their lives can still achieve wholeness even if they die in their sleep. Perhaps even a less agonizing death happens to those who are already transforming.

We know that the dying go through a kind of hell, a hell of letting go of themselves and their known lives. This is the constant battle for those who are dying, to let go of life and merge into death, to bring all to resolution.

One of the people who worked with me had a close relationship with her husband who was slowly dying over several years. Together they participated in his living his dying process with many rich results and transformations. Finally his health had so deteriorated that he was in the hospital in a coma and not recognizing anybody. She came to me and we talked. He seemed like he could last days, even weeks. His breathing was good, as were his vital signs. But the doctors did not think that he would ever become conscious again. I suggested that he might be hanging on and needed release, that maybe she and the five children could visit him that night in the hospital and say goodbye. She left not wanting to do this, feeling that he would live many days yet. But a friend heard the story and urged her to say goodbye that night. So she went with each of the children, one by one, and they said goodbye to their Dad. When they got home half an hour later the hospital called to inform them that he was dead. That is the way death works. It is the final releasing, and carries with it all the power of the most sacred of events, especially when we are in tune and honor its mystery.

In dying we are letting go. We are building character, often experiencing more pain than pleasure. We symbolize some process we are working through, often unconsciously. When we die slowly we constellate the victim archetype, drawing people to us. The people are attracted because the dying one symbolizes their own hidden vulnerability. The spectators participate in the dying process to experience their own dying. As you die, whenever you die, you can be aware of what you are constellating for others as well as what is being evoked for yourself. The following questions are suggestions for working with the dying experience. First, questions to ask of yourself, if possible in journalwork or in a meditative state. There are also questions to ask those who visit you to form a basis for dealing consciously with the energy being evoked. And then there are questions for visitors to ask of the one who is dying. Not bad. Don't just bring flowers to the relationship. Bring also the best questions you can.

Questions To Ask Yourself When You Are Dying

* What is actually happening to me at the present time? What are my fears and hopes? What is my reality?
* What is happening in my inner world at this time? Dreams? Feelings? Images? Insights?
* What is the purpose of this happening to me at this time?
* What needs resolution at this time in my life?
* What is the dying like? What does it evoke for me? What is my resistance to it? What do I need to do to deal with the whole experience?
* What are all the things I need to begin letting go of and how will I do it?
* What is the nature of healing in this situation?
* Am I ready to live as well as die?
* What are my choices, and what is my reality?
* How do I seem to be symbolizing death?
* What can I do to help others face their own dying process?
* What are the most meaningful final acts I can do and accomplish?

Questions You Can Ask of Others Who Visit You When You Are Dying

* What do I symbolize for you? What do you see in me? What do I evoke for you?
* What can you give me now that I don't already have?
* Have you made out your own will yet? Are your affairs in order as mine need to be?
* What do you want from me that you have come?
* Tell me about your own fears of dying?
* What would you like me to share about myself?
* What are you feeling right now?
* Am I the one you have come to visit or is it really a projection of yourself you see in my state? How are you living through me? What do you know of me individually?
* What do you want from me today? What are you projecting onto me today?
* What are your fantasies about me and my situation?
* What do you feel I most need in this situation that I am not able to see for myself?
* Have you had any dreams about me or about death?

Questions for a Visitor to Ask of Someone Who Is Dying

* How do you feel about my coming here today?
* What would you like from me?
* What is going on with you right now?
* What has happened for you since we shared last?
* What dreams have come to you in sleep?
* What is it like to be dying?
* What are your thoughts about death now, being in the condition you are in?
* What can you tell me about dying when my own turn comes around?
* What would you like from me the next time I come to visit you?
* What visionary experiences have you had, if any?
* How are you maintaining consciousness about this whole experience?

The Practices

1. What was your earliest experience of death and dying? What effect did this experience have on you?

2. What are your beliefs about death? What are the issues involved in your beliefs? In the death experience itself?

3. What are the archetypes involved in death? How are you relating to them?

4. What principles and practices do you have for dealing with death and dying? What would be some relevant ones from this book?

5. Have you made out your will or revised it recently? If not, why not? Plan to get your will made or current within a month.

6. Have you made the commitment to live life consciously and fully? Are you still afraid to die? **Those fear death who have not lived life.** What incompleteness in your life causes you to fear death?

7. List the things it would be good to let die now in your life and make choices regarding them.

8. Are you more on the side of life or death? Or are they in balance for you, living both opposites fully?

9. What do the questions and issues presented in this section evoke for you?

"And Death shall have its own dominion."

Practice 27

THE MEDITATIVE DAY

"We have not been sufficiently schooled in the moment."

What would it really mean to live each day entire unto itself? Most of us much of the time are still caught in the previous day's issues, trying to catch up with what is happening here and now.

Why spend the rest of one's life catching up with oneself?

Just as great a trap is to escape the present moment with fantasies and projections into the future. All is not going well now or to our liking? Well, let me see, I can space out and fantasize what I would like to have happen in my life. At least that will give me some pleasure and relief.

We have not been sufficiently schooled in the moment. What happens, happens now. There is no tomorrow. We have said this before and we say it again. The joy is in being fully present to what is happening to us every moment of our day.

And yet if we were somehow fully present, would we not be wiped out by all the input we were getting? The tax man is only a phone call away. Civilization can go within half an hour at the push of a button. My finances can be ruined with one wrong move in a business situation. I'm caught in innumerable compulsions and I can't seem to get free of even one of them. Life is survival and that's about all I can do.

I love life but does life love me? Why doesn't it happen the way I would like it to? Am I asking for all that much? Why is it that I want so much more than I'm getting out of life?
Buried in the above descriptions is a medley of attitudes.

* I don't have what it takes to do more than survive in life.
* The future is not likely to be better than the past.
* I'm tired and barely have the strength to improve my lot.
* I'll never really get what I want out of life.

You have been introduced to the practices, ways of orienting to life and centering oneself in what is essential. Certain fundamental life principles have been suggested as the effective contexts out of which to live one's life. You have learned how to create affirmations and intentions for yourself. Some of the deeper techniques, such as dreamwork and dialoguing with inner parts, have been introduced. The values of working with a skilled therapist at certain times in your life have been outlined. The necessity for having a spiritual life, even if you do not feel you are religious, has been made clearer.

Yet something still is lacking. What is that? Always there is more, more to the mystery and the next moment. But here, as a way of bringing completion to this book, we focus now on the nature of the Meditative Day.

The Meditative Day

Each day is entire unto itself, and how we live each day determines how we live the whole of our lives. If I live my day haphazardly I will live my life breeding chaos on chaos. Yet if I live my day and my life too closely bound I will be narrowing the groove until I am squashed in mediocrity. Somewhere in between is the circle of intentionality, that which will bring fullness and resolution to each day of my life, so that when the end comes to my mortality it will indeed be a completion of that spiraling circle destined for me.

Why die when the work is not yet done, when one's purpose for living has not yet been achieved?

We die daily whether we have reached resolution in our day or not. Why not then look at each day as a complete whole in itself, so that when we are ready for sleep we have brought our twenty-four hours to resolution and gone into dream space released, purified, and open for what the creativity of night offers, and then to wake at dawn fresh and ready for the next of life's adventures.

Waking Up in the Morning

The Meditative Day does and does not begin with the waking in the morning. The real beginning was going into the sleep state. But still, many of us have a difficult time opening our eyes to what awaits us. We would sleep some more, shut our eyelids and wait until the last minute to move ourselves out of bed to the bathroom, a rush through the kitchen, a hop into the car, and arrival, still not awake, at work where consciousness is demanded of us.

Oh Mother, let me have my hot coffee, please, or my cigarette. Coffee is the Great Mother, the warm liquid earth sometimes laced with the young bride's milk. We need that warmth because we have not practiced resolving our previous day, nurturing ourselves. We want some state of regression, a stay of execution even, for we are not ready.

It goes far easier to resolve each day as it comes along so that we may be fully present to the new day which is.

We may also wake to the morning the same way we came into the world. Were we welcomed at birth with warmth, affection, and security? Or were we held up in bright lights in a room colder than the womb, slapped to make us breathe, covered with cloth instead of held against warm skin, and taken from our mothers instead of being held secure and at rest on her breast for hours to suckle the new found milk of paradise from a young mother's breast?

The right way to be born allows transition from the old into the new. The birth is hard, full of pain and pushing for the mother, and squashing and newness for the baby. Babies do not usually cry as they come out of the mother's vagina, so the passage to the new world must not be all that painful. The pain comes later, the shock of entry with a minimum of transition.

The art of the Meditative Day is the art of making transition.

Grab your coffee, your cigarettes, your phone calls, your anxiety, and run, but where are you running to? Slow down and walk, allow time to stay with the previous energy until you have made it conscious and can move on.

A life without transition is a life without reflection.

The Problem of Catching Up With Oneself

To be fully present in the now we must resolve what went on previously.

To resolve issues we bring them to consciousness, sort out the alternatives and choose among them. We cannot always resolve everything in our lives in a single day, but we can make our issues conscious. If I cannot resolve the whole problem, at least I can break it down into its next step so that I will not feel so overwhelmed with its totality.

We catch up with ourselves by not leaving things hanging. Always put off until tomorrow what you cannot do today, means handle what you can each day and let the rest go until the next occasion for choice.

Too often we go into sleep dragging our problems with us. Journal-work is excellent for clearing the mind. If you write your issues on paper, you will at least be getting them out of your head so that you can become more receptive and empty-headed about life. Often the writing itself will help bring resolution by stimulating new consciousness and avenues for choice.

The Practices

1. Before falling asleep spend a few minutes in **sitting meditation**, letting the events of the day and your feelings about them come up into your consciousness. No particular order is needed. You are opening yourself and letting your psyche dictate what is most important or needing resolving. Next, you may want to write out an issue or two in your journal, stating the issues and the alternatives and possible creative solutions. Then take action, make a small choice. You might want to ask for a healing dream on the subject, make a commitment to tackle the problem the next day, or whatever.

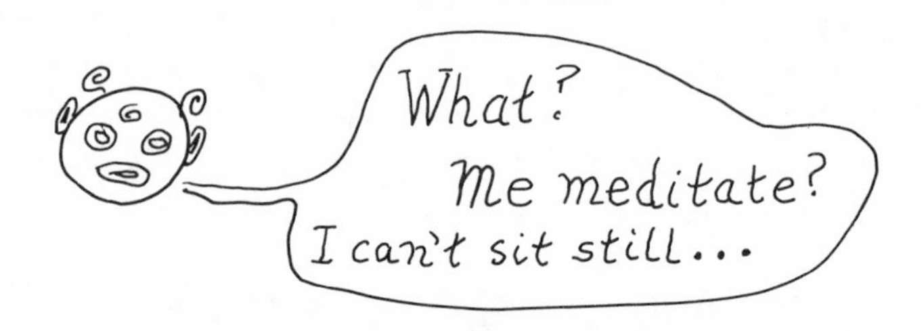
What?
Me meditate?
I can't sit still...

2. Some people also choose to **meditate with a lighted candle at their sacred area.** This has the affect of affirming center and giving a sense of transcendence and healing to one's life. However it is done, you might find yourself affirming center in some way, as with a prayer or a few thoughts sent to the world's victims as well as to those you hold most dear.

3. Just before sleep after your clearing meditation, think on what issue or potential you would like to have a dream about. Then enter sleep saying to yourself that you will wake remembering a dream or whatever else comes into your head. Upon awaking write down anything you are aware of without evaluating or censoring. You have been rewarded with a gift from the night, but it is not yours to choose what that gift will be.

4. Sleep itself is a **sacrifice**, a letting go of the ego into the unconscious. If you have not let go consciously you may have a difficult time yielding to sleep. In your in-between state practice letting go of all your issues, joys, anxieties, fears, feelings, images, whatever. And let go of your body as well, allowing it to find its own way of relaxation and rest. Tell yourself that all those cares will still be there tomorrow and there is absolutely nothing more you can do about them now. Live each moment of your life as it comes along. Do not project yourself into some future time as an escape from where you are now. Nothing matters as you drift away in your ship on its night sea journey.

5. In the **middle of the night** if you wake up, write down whatever is in your consciousness, maybe a dream, and then let it go. Do not try to force yourself to sleep. Let it happen, and if you are staying wide awake, write in your journal whatever thoughts are there, or do some other creative activity. Sleep will come when it comes. Your job is to practice yielding, not making happen.

6. **Upon waking** write down without thinking about it whatever comes into your head. Let it happen. Do not censor. Be with your thoughts in this most creative time for you. Make transition by staying with the night, yet moving into the dawn. After going to the bathroom you may want to do some sitting meditation, just to feel centered and more ready for your day. Then move into whatever you do next, again with no hurry even if you go with speed. Remember the transitions, relaxing into each moment, being aware of who you are and wherever you go.

7. Throughout your waking day, **practice meditation by consciously letting go to each moment as it comes up**, feeling its necessity and its potential, and feeling also your relation in your inwardness to what is happening. Remember that **there is always a creative solution to everything, and choices that can make it happen.** The resolutions to life's problems may not be what you thought or wanted, but healing resolutions will be there if you can perceive and actualize them. Do not remain identified with the moment, or with anyone or anything. You need your objectivity. You need to be involved, yet observing what is happening. You make yourself a vehicle for the process by opening up to it as it is. This is the Meditative Day, the essence of a centered life. And then you choose, accept the outcome, and never look back.

8. **Effect transition in whatever you do.** Lateness is often a symptom of not taking time, even if only for a few seconds, for renewal. Do not go from one activity to the next without a suitable transition. To make transition we bring to resolution what has just happened. We summarize. We find the essence. We make the final point. We also consult our own feelings. What was evoked for me and how am I dealing with it? I may have to act intuitively and quickly, but I work to not leave the essential hanging. This is the Meditative Day. Even as I enter a new room I pause to find out once again who I am, where I have been, and where I am going. Then having resolved, at least partially, what I have just been doing, I can move forward with openness and greet the next moment and people in my life, always seeking central values.

9. **Take periods of time for yourself** and your reactions throughout the day. Remember you are a person and have a right to exist as well as anyone else. If you are angry with someone for being lazy, maybe you are not relaxing enough yourself. You can identify with all your projects, your children, your roles, your fantasies, even, but none of this is the essential you. **You are a spark of consciousness finding itself in an unlimited universe.** Everything you do will be like drops of water in the rivers of life, or grains of sand in time's hour glass. Do not try to remain behind in any of these. You are a choice-maker moving forward in time. If you would achieve the essence and purpose of your life, you must try to do it in each moment where it counts, the only place it counts. You will know where you are going when you get there. Until then stay focused in the here-and-now to find its potential and the essence in all things.

10. And this is the Meditative Day. **All is energy, energy and form.** We learn to work the energy, to create with whatever comes up. This is our task if we would be effective in life. Stay with the energy, build with the energy, create with the energy, let go with the energy. And with this practice also is the **wholeness principle**. That in whatever you do, remember the opposites. Not, "just this," but "also this." When caught in one opposite we evoke the other opposite so that we may make choices which balance them and create new centers of wholeness. **To center means to affirm the whole, to have a circumference which is inclusive and total, allowing perfection and imperfection alike, and moving creatively onward with life.**

And so we include the facets of life in whatever we do, relationship, work, family, alone time, hardship, joy, fullness, the unexpected, the mystery, and meditative relation to the Source of All Life.

Reading List of Outstanding Books in The Field

The following list is not meant to be comprehensive, but serves to show the seminal works influencing this approach.

Memories, Dreams, Reflections, by C. G. Jung

The Inner World of Choice, by Francis G. Wicks

The Origins and History of Consciousness, by Erich Neumann

Man and His Symbols, by C. G. Jung, et. al.

The King and the Corpse, by Heinrich Zimmer

Puer Aeternus, by Marie-Louise Von Franz

Be Here Now, by Ram Dass

The Jungian-Senoi Dreamwork Manual, by Strephon Kaplan Williams

These are the classic works in the field. Someone else will have to comment on my own dreamwork manual cited here as a direct complementary volume to this one.

GENERAL PRINCIPLES

"Principles are not to be read but lived."

This is a list of principles articulated in the book. It is not intended to be complete or definitive. There may be several ways of stating a life principle. Try rewriting these, or writing out some of your own.

Adversary

1. The enemy is within.
2. There can be no hero without an adversary.
3. Victims are the adversary's heroes.
4. What I give is gone forever.
5. The more we hide from something the more it will attack us.
6. We are what we most fear.
7. I am my own anger. I am angry, ultimately, only at myself.

Adversity

8. What we most fear will happen to us one way or another.
9. We cannot avoid the negative by being positive.
10. We cannot flee the dark by fleeing to the light. We must bring light to our darkness and darkness to our light.
11. Love needs hate to exist.
12. What you try and leave behind will appear in front of you at the next gate.

Archetypes

13. The universe is continually created and re-created out of the archetypes which underlie it.
14. We identify with one archetype and project its opposite.

Attitudes

15. Making conscious and changing the attitudes which unconsciously control us leads to a transformed life.
16. Values are attitudes consciously realized.
17. Our traumas produce defense systems whose defenders are the attitudes we possess.

Change

18. To resist change is to create change in the extreme.
19. To change the part change the whole.
20. To change the world or those around you, change yourself first.
21. Every outer event is an inner opportunity to create change.
22. We must always be changing to meet a new reality.
23. It is by carrying out our intentions that we change life.

Choice

24. In order to choose Yes we must choose No to all that would oppose it.
25. In life there is neither absolute good nor absolute evil. There are only choices and their consequences.
26. Choice is the freedom to make conscious the inevitable.
27. We have free will only when we let go of the necessity to choose only one way.
28. We become what we choose. What we choose is what we become.
29. I have freedom only in my choices. I do not have freedom to determine the outcomes which result.
30. Most things can only be known after the choice is made, not before.
31. I always have choice in how I deal with situations.
32. I can consciously choose to let go of unconscious ways of reacting to life events.
33. A choice I can go back on is not a choice.

Conflicts

34. Conflicts are the battlegrounds of the opposites. All conflicts need differentiation and resolution eventually.
35. Trying to overcome power with power resolves no conflicts. It only makes them worse.

Consciousness

36. The Source needs consciousness to be actualized.

37. Nothing is real which has no consciousness attached to it.

38. You are a spark of consciousness finding itself in an unlimited universe.

39. Objectivity is created from objectifying one's subjectivity.

40. Knowledge must be tested by experience.

41. It is not what a person says but what they do which counts.

42. Compassion is no substitute for understanding.

43. Identification creates unconcsciousness.

44. Inner reality is prior to outer reality.

45. Destiny is what we make conscious.

46. We look inward to look outward.

47. Who I am determines how I live life.

48. We live out compulsively what we refuse to make conscious.

49. I must continually ask myself questions to become real.

50. I must doubt who I am to know that I exist.

51. The partners to all our thoughts and activities are their opposites.

52. We write to know ourselves.

53. What we share with others is really what we learn about ourselves.

54. Reflection upon life is what gives Life to life.

55. We talk to hear ourselves.

56. We dream to wake to life.

57. We identify with what we do and that makes us unconscious.

Death

58. To live, die daily to life.

59. We choose dying in order to live.

60. Those fear death who have not lived life.

61. Immortality is living fully in the now. In the now there is no death, and once the now is gone there is only death.

Effectiveness

62. Effectiveness is knowing the laws of reality and actualizing them.

63. A single focus on what could go well rather than badly leads to greater accomplishment in reality.

64. Do only what is essential in life and let the rest go.

65. Bringing consciousness to a situation makes us more effective in dealing with it.

66. Effectiveness is built out of accepting inadequacy.

67. There is always a creative solution to everything, and choices that can make it happen.

Ego

68. We do not have to choose death but we have to choose life.

69. Choice is the one absolute.

70. I deal with fear by letting go of what I am holding onto.

71. Striving to control life strangles life in us.

72. Letting go of control and serving the integrative source creates wholeness and meaning.

73. I give what I let myself receive.

74. To flee to the light is the greatest darkness.

75. It is not what we believe but what we do which determines our course in life.

76. The way out is always through.

77. To get what we want we must want what we get.

78. Fullness in life comes through letting go to life, not controlling it.

79. Always get your own house in order first.

80. Suffering purifies the ego for new life.

81. Better to not get enough than to get too much.

82. What you teach others is what you most need yourself.

83. We teach what we do not know.

84. The stronger the real ego as choicemaker is, the less egocentric it will need to be.

85. We defend ourselves from that which we are unwilling or unable to deal with and make conscious.

86. We isolate ourselves by what we do not share with others.

87. The wise person becomes strong in life not by simply going it alone but by seeking competent help whenever needed.

Fear

88. Identification with fear prevents action.

89. We dwell in insecurity to become secure.

90. You do not get over fear by living only love. You deal with fear by accepting and experiencing it fully.

Feelings

91. He who feels nothing fears all.

Fulfillment

92. Always want the process and let the goals take care of themselves.

93. In the long run it is more beneficial to meet one's own needs than to try and meet someone else's needs.

94. The more we reveal ourselves, the more we accept ourselves.

Healing

95. Sacrifice prepares us for healing and bringing resolution creates the healing.

96. Healing is bringing resolution to conflicts by harmonizing the opposites.

97. Go into and through the darkness for healing.

98. Healing comes through wholeness and individuation, and not self-will.

99. We heal others to heal ourselves.

100. The child is the healer of us all.

Heroic

101. There can be no adversary without a hero to fight with.

Life

102. What lives, lives now.

103. There are a thousand ways of saying "no" and only one way to say "yes" to life.

104. Life is the goal of life, and dying the process.

105. We choose life in order for it to choose us.

106. The secret of renewal is not collapse but change to a different way or area of self-expression.

107. Disidentifying from roles leads to transformation and new life.

108. I live because the universe wants life in me.

109. Life is living consciously.

110. We choose to live at the edge of risk.

111. When I let go of trying to control life, life can respond with healing and transformation.

112. The way to life is to let go of the past, to be fully present in the present so that the future may be born.

Love

113. Love is letting go of absolutes.

114. Love is the accepting and nurturing of the real.

115. Only that love is real which leads to a unity of opposites.

116. Love is the acceptance of each aspect of life in order to transform it by integrating it within the whole.

Opposites

117. He who feels joy must also feel pain.

118. The opposites exist to be differentiated and reconciled.

119. Identifying with one opposite causes the other opposite to come up and disidentify us.

120. Repressing an opposite causes it to come out as a compulsion.

121. Resolution means bringing opposites together to form a new unity.

122. The negative is as positive as the positive is negative. They are one whole.

123. Harmony is the balancing of opposing forces so that a new way different from each can emerge.

Principles

124. The universe rests on principles, the innate laws of the interrelations between things.

125. Effectiveness is built on knowing and actualizing the principles about how life and reality work.

126. I am a being who exists according to the innate principles of the universe.

Problems

127. There is always a creative solution to every problem in life.

Projection

128. We project what we have not yet made conscious.

129. We try and get others to do first what we most need to do ourselves.

130. Repression as well as identification causes projection.

131. I am the opposite I project.

132 We identify with one opposite and project the other.

Reality

133. Reality is healing.

134. Life is what happens now, not in the past or in the future.

135. Things will never go the way we want them to unless we both change what we want and want what comes our way.

136. Whatever happens is real.

137. Reality is the best medicine.

138. God is reality.

139. What is true is what is real.

140. Things will rarely go the way we expect them to in life. To expect the unexpected is reality.

Relationship

141. If you can say No in relationship you do not have to say No to the relationship.

142. Relationship is growing separately together.

143. Never keep a friendship longer than the potential to teach each other something.

144. We are born single to ourselves and we die utterly alone as well.

145. We relate to others to relate to ourselves.

146. One secret to successful relating is integrating the projections as they become known.

147. You have nothing to lose but yourself. You cannot lose another person.

148. The chief purpose of relationship is to effect change.

149. We seek relationship to find ourselves.

150. You do not seek relationship. You seek life and relationship will come.

Repression

151. Repression is the universal lie, the untruth of truth.

152. What we repress in one area will assert itself in another.

153. Wars are built on repression. Only those full of repressed anger want to kill someone.

Sacrifice

154. I choose in every moment to let go of that which would prevent living the greatest value in that moment.

The Self

155. Bringing resolution to conflicts of opposites creates new unities.

156. Unity is what holds existence together.

157. Dealing with conflict creates resolution and meaning.

158. In terms of destiny, we always have everything we need right where and when we need it.

159. We transform the negative with the positive. We transform the positive with the negative.

Sex

160. Sex will always be fresh where intimacy is achieved.

161. Sex is a gift, not a given.

The Shadow

162. We integrate the shadow by disidentifying from the persona and choosing wholeness.

163. To deal with your shadow, accept and create with its energy.

Spirituality

164. To become spiritual is to choose to do only those things which contribute meaning and healing to one's life.

Time

165. We do not save time. We spend it wisely.

166. The future is created out of what I do now, not what I do later.

Transformation

167. Transformation is total revolution in the psyche.

Wholeness

168. The goal of life is wholeness and the way to that goal is the practice of bringing resolution to all conflicts.

169. Ongoing wholeness is possible for anyone willing to pay the price of becoming conscious.

170. We must include both the positive and negative in life to achieve wholeness.

171. The journey means both letting go and integrating whatever comes up.

Epilogue

Let us reach out to each other, you and I, and form a circle of hands, hearts and choices. Let us become lights to ourselves and the world because we are practicing the conscious way, the way of integration, differentiation, and wholeness. Let us be clearly in the present where all potential for new life lies. Let us let go of the past with its outworn attitudes and memories. Let us welcome in the future with its tasks and potentials. Let us accept and transform darkness, not into light, but into unity of both the light and the dark, night and day, good and evil, the opposites entwined. Let us practice reconciliation and resolution in all things as our first principle for ourselves and for the world. Let us be winners all in the game of life as we pursue personal transformation in which there are no We and They but only a universal Us, a One World united in its achieving wholeness for itself and all individuals.

PART VI
SOURCES—SYNCHRONICITY READINGS FOR DEALING WITH LIFE'S ISSUES

Introduction

From time to time we all need perspective on the issues in our lives and the choices we make. We consult our own best values and perceptions, and we ask others for their advice and perspective.

The Source readings here, using synchronicity as the process, offer us still another context for consideration in making choices.

The ancients believed that there was a power or source guiding each person's life which you could relate to to fulfill yourself and understand your destiny. C. G. Jung called one of these sources the Self, the center within the psyche. He used the Chinese *I Ching, Book of Changes* as one of his tools for reflecting the wisdom of this inner source.

Jung coined the word *synchronicity* to describe the process of meaningful coincidence which is the basis of the *I Ching*. Synchronicity is when inner knowing unites with outer potential to produce a context for meaningful action. Those who follow this kind of intuitive knowing about one's potentials and dangers are often more creative and effective in life.

Like the *I Ching*, these Source readings use the principle of synchronicity. They came to the author in a meditative state sitting beside a wilderness river. They came spontaneously and they also represent years of working with people to help them achieve a sufficiently deep life perspective to handle their lives well. In a sense, these Source readings represent the possibility for wisdom in a situation. These readings may also reflect some psychic process of truly reading the potential of a situation. They may also read what is just under the surface of a person's consciousness, and so evoke new awareness which is already there but as yet unknown.

We cannot probe absolutely into how the readings work, or even how well they work. But you will probably obtain more meaningful responses the more you are open and focused on what you are dealing with.

Do not use these readings as the sole basis for choice. Only alive and human individuals make choices. You cannot let anyone else or any kind of psychic reading make your choices for you. They can add to or challenge your perspective, but in the end it is you, and you alone, who must choose what to do each step of the way in life. It is possible that you will receive a reading directly in contrast to your own perspective on a situation. You could reconsider your own position or use the other position as a test for your own.

The Source readings cannot be right or wrong. You do not use them to decide whom to marry, or where to invest your money. They simply challenge your perspective and help you enlarge your consciousness. You alone are making your choices and dealing with outcomes. Do not try to follow a reading literally. You will always be interpreting what you read. The best use of these Source readings is to increase consciousness, whether you believe a guiding force is at work in your life or not.

Sources–Synchronicity Readings for Dealing with Life's Issues is also published separately as a small book which can be carried in your pocket, your purse, or your backpack.

How to Obtain a Reading

1. Formulate your issues into an open-ended question rather than a Yes-No question. What perspective can you give me on this? rather than, Will I lose out if I do this in my life?

2. Respond to your own question. How would you answer it?

3. Choose a number from 1 to 64, using either the coin throwing method or the numbered deck method. In each case you obtain your number by chance with the assumption that if a guiding source is active in your life it will show itself through chance.

4. Look up your Source reading by number and let it affect you. What feelings are immediately evoked? What questions does it raise? How does it complement or challenge your own perspective?

5. When you use the coin throwing method, you may get two readings. The first may represent the present situation and the second the probable outcome. Or if the two readings seem to complement each other they will together give a stronger perspective on your situation. If the readings contrast they may be reflecting ambivalence in the situation.

6. Revise your perspective now and make your choice if the time seems ripe.

7. Write your issue question out, date it, and record the reading you received with its number. Write your comments and the choice you make. Later you might write the consequences of your choice in the light of the Source reading you received.

With either of these methods please stay focused on your issue question as you go through the process of obtaining your reading number.

The Coin Synchronicity Method

Throw three coins six times and record a sum number each time, using the values:

heads = 2 tails = 3

Three heads = 6, two heads and one tails = 7, two tails and one heads = 8, and three tails = 9.

Six and eight become broken lines (— —). Seven and nine become solid lines (——).

Six (— —) and nine (——) are changing lines, leading to a second reading.

Start at the bottom and work up, writing the number and the line for each toss of the coins. You are creating a **hexagram** made up of an upper and a lower **trigram.**

For example, if your first throw is three tails, your second two heads and one tails, and the other four throws are all two tails and one heads, your hexagram will look like this:

8 — — — —
8 — — — —
8 — — — —
8 — — — —
7 —— ——
9 —— → — —

Since nine is a changing line, you will have two hexagrams.

Now look at the chart. Your upper trigram is **light**, and your lower trigram is **unity**. So your first reading is number 19. The nine changing line gives you a second hexagram, whose number is 7.

The Numbered Card Method

Obtain a blank deck of cards from an educational supply store and write the numbers from 1 to 64 on the cards. Then close your eyes, shuffle the deck, pull out a card, and use the reading numbered thereon.

Synchronicity Source Reading Chart

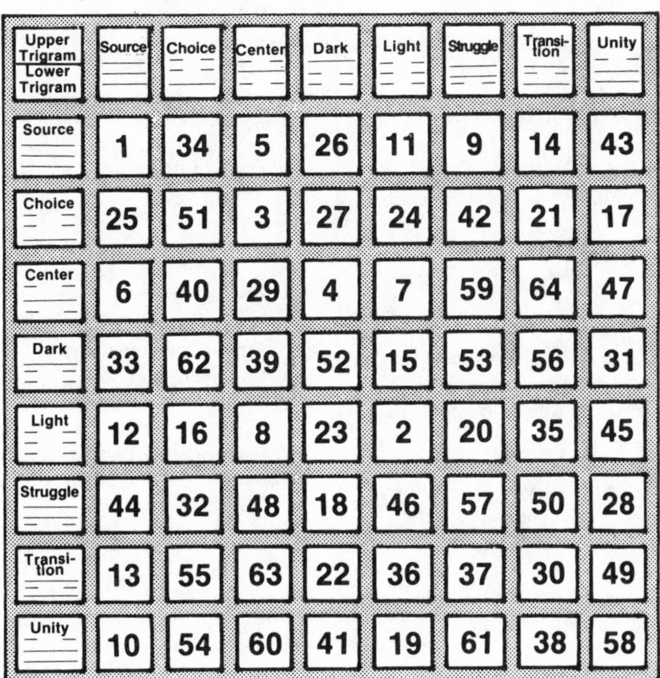

Upper Trigram / Lower Trigram	Source	Choice	Center	Dark	Light	Struggle	Transition	Unity
Source	1	34	5	26	11	9	14	43
Choice	25	51	3	27	24	42	21	17
Center	6	40	29	4	7	59	64	47
Dark	33	62	39	52	15	53	56	31
Light	12	16	8	23	2	20	35	45
Struggle	44	32	48	18	46	57	50	28
Transition	13	55	63	22	36	37	30	49
Unity	10	54	60	41	19	61	38	58

Heads = 2
Tails = 3

Three heads = — — → ——
Two heads, one tail = ——
Two tails, one head = — —
Three tails = —— → — —

Throw 3 coins six times. The first throw starts at the bottom and builds the Trigrams upward. Then look up the number for your reading.

1

You think your primary need in life is for love.

But have you considered that owning your own power is more where it is at?

We do not need love.

We need to choose love.

2

Why must you keep trying to be the center of attention?

What wound or need is making you express yourself inappropriately?

What you feel you need you already have.

We are most appropriate when we are most human.

Stay related to your own heart and things are more likely to work out well.

3

You do not seem to be able to get disinterested or disidentified with some problem to which you have become extremely attached.

The need for humor, and the cutting through it creates, would seem central.

Why do you take yourself all that seriously?

4

Your reserve in this situation is indeed becoming to you.

But without risking more and opening yourself to others you may never achieve a major aspect of your life.

Consider whether you are operating with true dignity or out of a defense system.

5

Your own wholeness is what is most important, whatever the outcome.

You have only one life to live. Why spend it trying to meet the expectations of others?

You know in your heart that you have only been defeating yourself.

The dance of life is in letting go to the true Self within.

6

From the beginning you have known that you have a single purpose to achieve in life.

Why be so loaded down in the morass and minor issues of experience?

Focus your energy.

Make the most central choices and you will succeed in what you are meant to do.

7

Success, or victory, is not yours at this time. You have, perhaps, more letting go to do.

Yes, things are at times difficult. But consider that you are now paying back what you have taken unconsciously.

The opposite of success is loss.

Balance must be achieved before your own wholeness can take a new direction.

8

If pleasure is your chief purpose, then you well might enjoy yourself in this situation.

But it will not ultimately be that which you long for.

Whatever you do, live passionately.

You can only find yourself by giving all to your process. Purity of intention is the true choice here.

What you seek may not come about.

Something better is on the way.

9

Things are in a decline.

Accept what is happening to you. Resistance will only weaken the opportunities you still have to achieve balance.

You have within your power the chance to achieve the essence of the situation.

Do not hold onto anything and your guides will indicate the way to go.

Decline is a time of letting go after maximum fulfillment. You may be starting another cycle.

10

Creativity would be a strong suggestion right now.

You are seeking answers rather than encompassing opposites.

Do not retreat into known values. Open yourself more to symbolic processes which tune you into resources beyond your rational thinking.

The solution to your problem must come out of the unknown.

11

Flowing and nurturing will enhance the situation to the fullest.

Do not identify with your goal or attempt to control anything.

A birthing process is at work with its own rhythm and outcome.

Acceptance and enhancing is required.

12

You are absolutely where you need to be.

Nothing more is needed in your life right now than what you already have.

Re-evaluate yourself and your situation so that you may become fulfilled using resources already available.

The only thing new needed is a change of attitude.

13

Why are you consulting once again?

You are being asked to change your point of view in the situation. What you give up will be more than compensated for by what you gain.

Relax, choose, and get it over with.

14

Confusion is a state of mind.

Even though the pieces of the puzzle do not seem to fit together right now, what is happening is exactly what you need.

Your way of looking at reality may be about to change. So relax and enjoy it.

There is always more adventure in the unknown than in the known.

15

Of course you are hurting, or at least bewildered.

Pain is our second nature, so why do you fight it?

Choose now to become more active with your own process.

Even make choices which will cause suffering so that you may strengthen yourself.

There is no truth which is harmless.

16

Happiness is a result, not a goal.

What is keeping you looking for happiness rather than accepting the positives which are present for you now?

Your tendency toward self-negation and perfectionism may be clouding your eyes to actual accomplishments.

What you already have is what you need.

17

Sorry, but you are perhaps too resistant to reality.

Do not ask why this is happening to you, but what can you creatively do about it?

Your ideals, or lost needs, still tend to get in your way. Reality, not fantasy, is where you must make your choices.

Shift radically your thinking so that you will be more accepting of life.

18

Reacting to things is better than passively going along with whatever comes your way.

But consider whether your rebelliousness is still being caught in others' values and expectations?

We become strong through finding our own values and resources in a situation.

Responding, rather than reacting, is the true necessity.

19

The situation is really not all you make it out to be.

In what ways might you be exaggerating in order to create an effect?

Your tendency to the dramatic may need to be counterbalanced by doing things at an everyday level which solve your own problems.

Intensity of feeling needs balance in objectivity and conscious choice-making.

20

Even though what you may seem to be experiencing is ending and dissolution, this is only the necessary stage for new life.

Do not escape the process but experience both aspects in their fullness.

Only then will you realize the next step.

The second birth comes out of death and rebirth.

21

Why not dance a little more on the light side of life?

Are you being a bit too serious in this situation?

Your tendency to identify with yourself as the center can prevent you from letting go to what is happening around you.

In the final analysis all is a game in which each of us is the ball but only one of the players.

22

Stop thinking and feel.

There is no way out but through.

Too much rational thinking keeps the problem abstract. In your heart you know what is right. But your fear of a new and different outcome distances you from the situation. Seek the place of greatest energy and there will be that with which to deal.

Outer problems reflect inner necessities.

Until you learn this principle you will be groping in the darkness of your mind.

23

Are you being too hysterical in this situation?

Feelings are not everything. Choice and objectivity are also necessary to any real solution.

Relax and take things one at a time. Even list the alternatives and their values.

And when the time is ripe, choose without dramatics or overly involving others.

24

What is the big hurry?

What may be more needed in the situation is time and letting go.

You already have the solution as part of your destiny.

But to force an outcome before the natural transition would simply create further agony.

Accept the uncertainty in the situation and ground yourself, one day at a time. When the time is ripe to act you will know it because of a sense of inevitability.

Fate creates us but we create destiny through choice.

25

A wonderful sense of wholeness may be developing for you.

Are you entering a time in which things are really falling into place?

What you have longed for is about to be achieved, at least for this stage of your life. But ask yourself how committed and responsible are you willing to be?

In order to achieve abundance we must study the situation well and act assuredly to actualize the fullest potentials.

26

The relationship is not as you would like it, but it is the relationship you have, so deal with it.

Ultimately, every relationship is with ourselves. So what you are learning here, despite the difficulties, can only accrue to your benefit.

Relationship is more your ability to relate than what happens to you.

27

Perhaps you are not where you belong at the present time?

What you have going is too confining.

A change is needed.

If you do not act, the decision will be made for you and with perhaps difficult consequences.

How much better to act when the time is ripe than after, when the consequences are already coming in.

28

Perhaps how you define the issue is too limited.

Consider the totality and the purpose for your life.

Develop also a sense of destiny, or life lived within a framework of meaningful values.

It is the journey which carries us through all the specifics of life.

29

Your safety is at stake.

Choose carefully and seek help.

What you do in the situation may tip the scales in one direction or another.

Be more concerned about yourself than others at this time.

Take care of the details and the larger totality will become known.

30

Your spiritual and psychological sources are at a prime.

What you are meant to achieve is now happening for you.

Maintain objectivity and a strong sense of devotion.

Your life is no longer your own.

But fullness is assured if you continue to develop the path you are now going.

31

Helplessness is not your best trait.

Ask yourself whether or not you are mostly indulging in old pains and misfortunes which are no longer relevant.

The best cure is a change of attitude which affirms purpose in your life.

Thinking of yourself alone, and not a larger spiritual journey, will keep you dependent on your own fears and the resources of others.

32

The past is dead.

Open yourself to the future.

Let go of old ties and ways of looking at things. Your better self lies in what you can yet become.

But in order to achieve your next stage in life it will be more necessary than ever to focus your energies through sacrifice of the unessential and choosing only that which fulfills the central purposes of your life.

33

Communication is not as it could be in this situation.

Much more needs to be known to all parties involved. It might well be important to speak forthrightly and leave nothing to chance.

Keeping things hidden only makes the situation worse.

Communication is a giving, not a withdrawing process.

34

Are you really grounded in what you are setting out to do?

Do you have a tendency here to leap ahead and avoid important details?

Focus on what is possible at the present time and determine if that is your priority.

If not, sacrifice what you thought you wanted and open yourself to what might really be the central issue.

35

You see yourself as willing, but commitment might be lacking.

Cure any innocence you have left by considering more the consequences. Then enter a process of active choice-making by becoming decisive in the situation and choosing for your highest values.

Commitment is a sustained choice over a definite period of time to achieve a specific goal or value.

36

You are maybe not active enough yet in the choice-making process?

Consider the alternative.

Consider the consequences.

Consider the context of attitudes and values within which you are making a choice.

Then choose by saying Yes to one thing and No to all which would oppose it.

37

Consider whether the regressive pull is at work.

An innate force within ourselves and in life wants to either hold us where we are or pull us back into the past with its outworn attitudes and values. We resist this tendency towards negation in the face of the new by discipline, commitment, and active choice-making.

New life is calling. What will be your response?

38

What you seem to be needing right now is a good dose of reality.

Your fears are perhaps exaggerated and your hopes too inflated.

Ground yourself by taking one day at a time. Practice accepting and dealing with whatever comes your way.

Reality is all you have, is all any of us have as the arena within which to live life.

39

Innocence is not in your best interest.

Your ability to protect yourself is at a low ebb. To regain equilibrium assert as much mastery in the situation as possible.

You must know your own heart and mind.

To follow the direction of others only brings disaster in the long run. Strengthen your freshness of purpose with skills and knowledge based on direct experience.

You have nothing to lose but your limitations.

40

Your resources are flowing, so why not use them to full advantage?

Too limiting a self image can now begin to change as you more fully come into your own.

What you have seemed to lack for so long is now being given you.

You have only to guide and make conscious the energy in order to achieve success at this stage.

41

Your spiritual life would seem to be lacking.

You are maybe too set in traditional attitudes and in letting others determine life's values.

It would be best to act now in developing spiritual practices.

You are ready for establishing relations with sources greater than yourself.

The next phase of your life will include that of being a seeker.

42

Help is on the way.

You have only to endure a little longer your deep suffering.

Remain steadfast in your search for healing.

Acknowledge that even in the worst of situations choice rules the day if it is made within a context of the ultimate meaning of your life.

43

Seek center and transformation in all that you do.

The externals of life are simply the web. At the center is the transformative power of the Self.

Check to see if you are following only your own knowledge and wants in the situation.

Or are you seeking even more to realize what your deepest sources want from you?

Therein will you be achieving wholeness.

44

Prepare for ending.

The final resolution is now possible.

Let go to what most needs to happen in you and in the situation.

Allow everything and achieve the essence of what is actually happening.

There is no turning back.

There is only the arrival at center.

45

The opposites are seeking a reversal in your life.

What was valid for you has become too one-sided and now you must go more to the opposite to achieve a balance point.

The final goal is living at the center, not at the extremes.

46

What is needed is commitment and courage.

The situation will not be overcome unless you risk everything in the struggle.

If you are unwilling to push through you will suffer a loss anyway.

Maximum effort and devotion may well tip the scales in a favorable direction.

47

Decisiveness and structuring may well be necessary to dealing with the issue.

Focus your energy and your choice-making and act with a sense of purpose and finality.

Your focus must become clear through action.

48

Are you still resisting suffering in the situation?

Suffering is the pain you feel from blocking or not yielding to the process.

Your pain may be the pain of not letting go of old habits and values.

Seek help and support so that you may open yourself within a circle of security and caring.

49

You may be moving into a major relationship.

But remember that every relationship is major if we make it conscious. What may be needed now is a sense of pacing. Eagerness can be balanced with objectivity. Trying to make things happen the way you would want can be offset by practicing a sense of flow.

It all happens when it happens.

And what happens, happens now.

50

Adversity must have its say.

Allow the dark side to come up so that it may be known and therefore better dealt with.

Prepare against being overwhelmed. Work within an active process of commitment to healing.

Adversity creates the challenge to include one more side of ourselves and life.

51

You will not find the solution to your problem here.

It may be that there is no solution right now to what you are dealing with?

What may be called for is choice, not endless weighing of positive and negative.

Keep choosing and never look back.

It is better that you deal with consequences than dilemmas.

52

Yes, you are faced with unutterable darkness. Not only the unknown besets you. You are also coping with potentially destructive forces.

Strengthen your commitment to living a conscious, healing life. Stay grounded in the little things of the everyday world. Do not subject yourself directly to intense forces. What is naturally happening is enough. Even darkness is healing if we accept and deal with it.

53

Perhaps you have not really found yourself yet?

Consider how you may be reacting to the expectations of others. Maybe you are still being governed by attitudes and reactions developed in childhood? You will not find your essential nature and what you're meant to be until you have fully rooted up the childhood woundedness and the defensive patterns it has caused.

Healing means going through to the other side.

54

Seeing outside what is really within may be of central concern in this issue.

What are you projecting into the situation which would best be taken as your own problem and potential?

Your heart is full, but feelings may need to be translated into actions.

55

You are already in a tremendous transition growth period in your life. Maintain stability through ongoing conscious work.

The danger is that you will let go too soon and seek rest before the process has reached its culmination.

The period of maximum choice is at the height of fullness.

Let your passion match your good fortune.

56

You may be dealing with a death in your life right now. The best preparation is to already be active in the letting go process.

Your fear of death is really your fear to live life to the fullest.

57

Compulsion has got you in its grip. You would be free to choose, yet your anxieties keep you bound and defenseless.

Ask what hidden needs you are serving when you compulse. Ask also whether you are willing to risk the natural suffering to which you are entitled?

Within your fears is true healing. You have only to let go to what you would avoid. But within the letting go maintain a balance and direction.

That which you secretly serve can now become conscious. What we most fear is what we most need.

58

Going fast will not get you anywhere.

We go fast by going slow.

What is needed is direct involvement in the situation, not rising above it.

Are you one who would spare yourself the drudgery of going through the valleys by leaping from mountaintop to mountaintop?

Slow down by taking one step at a time. Relish the details and what seems insignificant. Where you are going is where you already are.

59

You are perhaps not quite yourself.

Great energies are moving in your life. Any tendency toward ecstasy and identification with sources other than yourself may overwhelm you and ultimately cause despair.

Your authenticity is at stake. Come to yourself and your true humanity. Accept the ordinariness of life. The arena of living is in matter. Choose to integrate what is happening to you by making it conscious.

60

Limitation is true freedom.

What you are experiencing is what you are meant to achieve. Complaining and avoidance will not get you anywhere. What you have to deal with you carry with you. Through limitation we accept what is, in order to go deep.

What may be required of you is a sacrifice. Consider being more contained.

Where expansiveness and creativity are overdominant, reality is healing.

61

Be content with your lot.

62

Life is a game of life.

Why not learn to play more with circumstances?

You may be too identified with the present to create the future.

Free yourself from too much seriousness by letting go of all necessities.

Allow tensions to develop, and create with the energies evoked.

63

Everything is just as it should be.

You have little to be so worried about. You have made progress, and the path you are on is a true one.

Go over recent experiences and obtain their essence. You will see how much progress you have made, especially in the little things.

What matters most is a realistic image of yourself in which the positive balances the negative and wholeness asserts itself.

64

You may be entering a period in life when your ability to choose new direction can be especially enhanced.

Clarify your purposes and discard forcefully old ways and relations.

At the horizon new potential waits.

Action is required.

THE CHIEF REFERENCES ON SYNCHRONICITY

"Synchronicity: An Acausal Connecting Principle" in The Collected Works of C. G. Jung, Vol. 8, **The Structure and Dynamics of the Psyche**, Princeton University Press

C. G. Jung's forward to **The I Ching or Book of Changes** by Wilhelm and Baynes, Pantheon Books

---

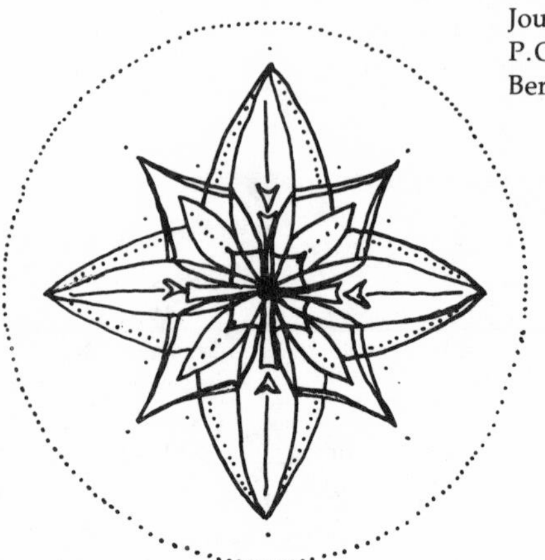